Leader's Guide to
The Relaxation & Stress Reduction Workbook

Fourth Edition

Martha Davis, Ph.D

New Harbinger Publications, Inc.

Publisher's Note

This publication is designed to provide accurate and authoritative information in regard to the subject matter covered. It is sold with the understanding that the publisher is not engaged in rendering psychological, financial, legal, or other professional services. If expert assistance or counseling is needed, the services of a competent professional should be sought.

Copyright 1995 Martha Davis
New Harbinger Publications, Inc.
5674 Shattuck Avenue
Oakland, California 94609

Copyedited by Mary McCormick

ISBN 1-57224-036-9 Softcover

Distributed in the U.S.A. primarily by Publishers Group West; in Canada by Raincoast Books; in Great Britain by Airlift Book Company, Ltd.; in South Africa by Real Books, Ltd.; in Australia by Boobook; and in New Zealand by Tandem Press.

Third Edition
First printing July 1989 2,000 copies
Second printing May 1990 2,000 copies
Third printing June 1992 1,000 copies
Fourth printing April 1994 1,000 copies
Fourth Edition
First printing, 1995 2,000 copies

Preface

This guide was specifically designed to assist you in leading groups, using *The Relaxation & Stress Reduction Workbook*. It tells you

- the salient points in teaching stress reduction and relaxation.

- which are the most important exercises to cover, and which are optional.

- a logical order for presenting the exercises.

- the length of time needed for each exercise.

- what materials are needed for each exercise.

- how to integrate *The Relaxation & Stress Reduction Workbook* audiotapes into your program.

- several formats for different lengths of groups.

- the typical problems people encounter when first learning these techniques and suggestions for resolving them.

- how to adjust exercises to fit your group size and environmental specifications.

- how to give clear homework assignments.

- how to review homework in group.

- how to use resistance as a teaching tool.

- how to motivate students to do their homework and continue to use these techniques when the group is over.

This guide assumes that you are already familiar with *The Relaxation & Stress Reduction Workbook,* so it will not repeat the basic concepts and step-by-step instructions found there. For best results, have your students read the workbook as the text used for your class or workshop.

The short lectures and exercises you give them in class will then be reinforced by their reading at home.

It is important for you to add material that is of particular interest to you and to your specific group. This will bring special meaning and vitality to the material, and will keep the group and you fresh and involved.

Refer to the bibliography at the end of each chapter in the workbook. Feel free to experiment with and expand upon the material presented here and in the workbook.

Contents

1

Introduction to Relaxation and Stress Reduction

One of the best ways to begin the class is to introduce yourself; talk briefly about how you became interested in the field of stress management and relaxation, what experience you have in teaching this subject, and why you think this is an important topic for the people in your class.

Stress and the Stress Response

Your introduction leads naturally into a brief lecture on stress and the stress response. Be sure to highlight the basic concepts of Chapter 1 in the workbook and include points of relevancy for your particular audience.

   Time: 30 minutes

Special Notes

Here are several important points to keep in mind when you give a lecture to the class:

1. The three major purposes of a lecture in this context are **to inform, to clarify misconceptions,** and **to motivate.**

2. Give new information in small chunks so that people can easily assimilate.

3. Keep your message simple. The average audience will not be interested in nor remember more than a few cited research studies. While you will want to provide some historical context and scientific basis for the importance of stress management and relaxation, you will lose a lot of people if you give them an academic treatise.

4. Gear your message to the educational level and interests of your audience.

5. Make your message encouraging. Cite personal or clinical anecdotes and studies which indicate that your concepts are grounded in experience and that your techniques work.

6. Provide an opportunity for class members to ask questions. It's best if you let people know before you start lecturing whether you want to answer their questions as you go along or at the end of your talk.

7. Make it clear before you start answering questions that the purpose of a stress management and relaxation class is to teach general concepts and techniques which have universal relevancy, and not to address the details of an individual's particular life situation. It is hoped that in the process of learning these general skills the individual will solve many of his own specific problems or clarify the need for one-on-one professional help.

8. Since the individual student will relate to the general concepts and techniques in terms of his specific situation, he will often bring up questions and comments particular to his life experience. This can benefit him and the class as long as it throws further light on the basic stress management concepts and exercises. It is important for the leader to interrupt people who want to talk at length about their symptoms and problems. You can relate these individual examples to general stress management concepts, and then redirect the class to stress management skill building. Examples of how to do this are as follows:

   "That brings up an important point, Mrs. Cook." Then follow up this statement with how her problem or symptom is a good example of stress or a stress response.

   *

   "You sound pretty discouraged, frustrated, and angry about the unfair treatment you are getting at work. What stress management tools have you learned thus far that you think might help you deal more effectively with your reaction to this stress?"

   *

   "You must be my straight man today, John, I was just about to bring up the topic of 'Job Stress.'"

   *

   "Betty, I know that your husband and children really get on your nerves, and you have discovered that the stress reduction technique of just talking about it reduces your frustration level and tension headaches. Rather than use the group to ventilate your feelings, I'd like to see you begin to make some new friends with whom you can share your feelings and get emotional support. Social networks serve as a buffer against the stresses of life."

9. At some point during the first session, you may want to give the class logistical information. This information can be in written form and referred to in as little or much detail as you prefer. Typical logistical information includes:

   - the name of your class or workshop

- your name
- when the class session is to begin and end
- the total number of sessions
- the date of the last session
- holidays when the class will not meet
- when you plan to take a break during the session
- location of rest rooms and smoking areas
- your expectations regarding confidentiality
- your expectations regarding audiotaping
- your expectations regarding attendance and punctuality
- your expectations regarding class participation
- your expectations regarding homework assignments
- instructions regarding how to get credit for the class
- requirements for those taking class for credit
- name of text and where it can be purchased
- list of topics to be covered
- the learning modalities to be used:

    lecture

    demonstration of exercises

    practice exercises in class

    discussion and questions

    practice exercises at home

    monitoring your own experience and progress

    reading text at home

    audio cassette tapes

10. At this point, the group members are clear about what they are going to learn, why you think that it is important, and how you intend to conduct the class.

Exercise: Schedule of Recent Experience

Purpose:

1. Allows individuals to get acquainted.

2. Enables individuals to acknowledge to themselves and others the major stresses in their lives.

3. Underscores the relationship between cumulative stress and the possibility of major illness.

Time: 30 minutes

Materials: If students do not have their own copies of *The Relaxation & Stress Reduction Workbook* yet, give each group member a copy of the Schedule of Recent Experience sheets on pages 5 to 9. Provide extra pencils or pens for those who do not have one.

Instructions:

1. You can use the introduction to the Schedule of Recent Experience on page 5 in the workbook. Remind the class that one definition of stress is "any change to which you have to adjust."

2. Go over the instructions on pages 5 through 9 in the workbook, and then answer questions.

3. Tell students to raise their hand if they have a question as they go along, and you will come over and assist them.

4. Instruct students who finish early to get up and take a break without disturbing those who are still working.

5. When everybody is finished scoring the inventory, call the class back to order.

6. If you are working with a large group, have students break into small groups of three or four people, introduce themselves, and share what they have learned about themselves in taking the Schedule of Recent Experience. Have one person in each group volunteer to later report back to the large group anything particularly interesting or any unanswered questions that come up in his group. (If you are working with a small group, you can ask each person to share in turn.)

7. Two minutes before the end of the allotted time, give people a two-minute warning to wrap it up.

8. Have the small groups reassemble into one large group. Then ask each one of the small group reporters to share what his group learned that was particularly interesting and any questions that remained unanswered. During this discussion, be sure that the following points are covered:

   • Changes can be big or small, positive and/or negative.

   • Having to adapt to change is stressful.

   • The stress of change is cumulative.

   • The amount of change a person experiences may be predictive of future illness.

   • People vary in their perception of a given life event and their ability to adapt to it.

- Just because a person received a high score doesn't mean that he has to get sick; the individual can do many things to help prevent illness and stay healthy.

Other points to include:

- The range of scores given for the Schedule of Recent Experience is based on a hospital population. Persons who received high scores were people who tended to get sick more frequently than people with low scores. This is only a correlation. Critics of the Schedule of Recent Experience would argue that it does not necessarily show cause. There are many other factors that contribute to whether a person is likely to become ill, such as genetic predisposition, stabilizing influences (i.e., a good social network, a pleasant home life, a satisfying job, a regular exercise program), and how people perceive the stresses in their lives and their ability to respond to those stresses.

- Typically, there will be a few participants who will score low on the Schedule of Recent Experience but who are ill or worn out. Have these people fill out the inventory again, this time for the year preceding the past year. It is likely that their second score will be higher than their first. A frequent comment from these people is that they really needed this class one or two years ago, but were too busy just trying to survive.

- Given that we cannot go back and re-choose our parents, stress management focuses on what we do have some control over: our thoughts, feelings and behavior, and to a lesser extent our environment.

Symptom Checklist

Purpose:

1. This inventory will help individuals identify their stress symptoms and decide how uncomfortable each of these symptoms are.

2. At the end of class, students can fill out the checklist a second time to determine how much symptom relief they were able to achieve with the tools they learned in this class.

Time: 10 to 20 minutes

Instructions:

1. See pages 10 and 11 in the workbook.

2. This inventory can be filled out in class or given as homework.

3. After your students have completed this inventory, call for questions and comments.

4. *Optional:* Read off the symptoms and have people raise their hand if they gave themselves a three or higher on a particular item. This is useful information for you. It will also give your students a sense that they are not alone in their particular brand of suffering.

5. *Optional:* Let people form dyads to briefly discuss their symptoms of stress. Limit this to about four minutes.

Symptom Effectiveness Chart

Purpose:

1. This chart gives a rough overview of the most effective stress management and relaxation techniques for relieving specific symptoms.

2. This is an excellent way to give a quick overview of what you plan to cover in your course.

3. It is interesting to review this chart with the class at the last session, asking individuals which tools they thought were most useful in relieving their stress symptoms. This can be done efficiently with a show of hands. This discussion provides useful information for you to consider how you will improve your classes in the future.

Time: 5 minutes

Instructions:

1. See pages 14 and 15 in the workbook.

2. Show your students how to read the chart.

Note: While the techniques that are most effective in treating a specific symptom are marked with an "X," students must take into account their individual situation in deciding which tools will help them. For example, Lonnie's major symptom of stress is obesity due to compulsive eating. Obviously, she needs to work on nutrition and exercise. But she also needs to ask WHAT TRIGGERS her compulsive eating. If she eats because she is a perfectionist who often fails to achieve her high expectations, she needs to look at "Refuting Irrational Ideas" (Chapter 14). If she eats because she has difficulty saying "no" to people, asking directly for what she wants, dealing with criticism from others, or expressing her feelings and opinions, then she needs some "Assertiveness Training" (Chapter 17). If she tends to give up her diet or exercise program at the first temptation or hardship, she will benefit from "Coping Skills Training" (Chapter 15). If she eats to relax and dampen her anxiety, then she would benefit from learning relaxation techniques. The Stress Awareness Diary, in "Body Awareness" (Chapter 2), is a useful tool for students who want to learn more about what triggers their symptoms of stress.

2

Body Awareness

Exercise: Body Inventory

Purpose: Promotes awareness of body, especially tension areas.

Time: about 25 minutes

Instructions:

1. See pages 17 to 19 in the workbook.

2. Give a brief introduction to Body Awareness.

3. *Optional:* Play the 21-minute New Harbinger Publications audio cassette tape on Body Inventory, which will take the class through the following three exercises: Awareness, Body Scanning, and Letting Go of Your Body.

4. Take the group through the Internal versus External Awareness exercise, one step at a time.

5. Go directly on to the exercise on Body Scanning.

6. Make it clear that people do not need to close their eyes to do this exercise; it just makes it easier to focus inward. Some people are fearful of closing their eyes around strangers. A few are even fearful of closing their eyes when alone at home to do something new such as these exercises.

7. Be sure to give people enough time to follow one instruction before moving on to the next one. A good way to judge this is by doing the exercise along with the class.

8. *Optional:* After completing the first two awareness exercises, have members of the group turn to a person sitting next to them and share what they became aware of that

they were not aware of before doing the exercises. Give each person a minute or so to respond.

9. The exercise on Letting Go of Your Body does not require participants to lie down. If they are sitting in chairs, specifically instruct them to take everything off their laps, rest their feet flat on the floor, and put their hands in their laps. Invite them to close their eyes, if they wish. Follow the instructions in the workbook, remembering to allow ample time for people to comply.

10. After completing the Letting Go of Your Body exercise, have group members turn to the person sitting next to them and share what they became aware of that they were not aware of before doing this exercise. Give each person a minute or so to respond.

11. Call for questions and comments.

12. These three exercises are presented in this order because they build on one another and ask the participant to do progressively more challenging things. The exercises can, however, be presented separately or in conjunction with other relaxation exercises. If you have time to do only one of these exercises, do Body Scanning.

13. Encourage people to practice these three Body Inventory exercises each day on their own. Good times to practice are when they go to bed, before getting up in the morning, when they are having to wait, during a work break, or any other naturally occurring lull during their day when they are free to turn their attention inwards. The other option is to schedule an appointment with themselves to do a Body Inventory each day at a particular time.

14. Tell members to use the Record of General Tension described on workbook page 21 to keep track of their tension level before and after they do Body Inventory exercises. In this way, they can monitor their progress and remind themselves to do the exercises regularly.

15. *Optional:* Have your students use the Record of General Tension to monitor their progress on all relaxation homework assignments.

Exercise: Stress Awareness Diary

Purpose:

1. The diary is a homework tool that allows students to monitor their awareness of their symptoms and stresses throughout the day.

2. The diary identifies how particular stresses result in predictable symptoms.

Time: 5 minutes to explain in class

Materials: several pieces of paper and a pen or pencil

Instructions:

1. Have the participants follow the instructions in the workbook on pages 19 and 20.

2. Many people find that it is excessive to keep the diary for two weeks. Students who keep a diary for two or three days during a week and one day on the weekend net some very useful data. For this exercise, it is best to set a minimal expectation for homework, and let people exceed it.

3. Tell your students that they will have an opportunity to go over their Body Inventory exercises and Stress Awareness Diary at the beginning of the next session.

4. Start the next session by having participants gather in groups of three or four to discuss how each person fared with the assignments.

   - Instruct the people who did their assignments to describe any connections they observed between specific stresses in their lives and their symptoms of stress. Ask them also to comment on their experience with the Awareness exercises and their Record of General Tension.

   - See Chapter 22 in this guide for suggestions on how to deal with people who do not do their homework.

   - Have one member from each small group report on how many people did the homework, and any interesting observations or unanswered questions when the large group is reconvened.

3

Breathing

Exercise: Breathing Awareness and Deep Breathing

Purpose:

1. Enables a person to discover how he currently breathes.

2. Points out the most obvious bad breathing habits.

3. Develops awareness of how the chest, diaphragm, and abdomen each play a role in the breathing process.

4. Facilitates deep, relaxing breathing.

Time: 15 minutes

Instructions:

1. Perhaps because people take breathing for granted, beginning with a lecture on breathing is a waste of time. Skip right to the exercise on Breathing Awareness.

2. Follow the instructions for the Breathing Awareness exercise on pages 25 and 26 in the workbook. Ideally, this exercise should be done lying down, in loose clothing, and on a blanket or rug on the floor. If this is not possible, have participants do the exercise in their seats.

3. Move around the room to make sure that people have their hands placed correctly. Share your observations regarding individuals' breathing patterns (i.e., breath holding, shallow chest breathing, and deep abdominal breathing). Invite questions and comments.

4. After your students are all aware of how they typically breathe, demonstrate Diaphragmatic, or Abdominal, Breathing while in a sitting and lying down pose. Place one hand on your chest and one hand on your abdomen, exhale deeply, pause, and

inhale slowly. Exaggerate the movement so that it is easy for your students to see. Demonstrate pressing down on your abdomen as you exhale to force air out. When you are lying down, rest a book on your abdomen to illustrate exhalation and inhalation. Note that Diaphragmatic Breathing is generally easier to practice initially when lying down, and that they can experiment with the lying down and sitting up poses at home.

5. Instruct your students to shift to Diaphragmatic, or Abdominal, Breathing by exhaling completely, pausing a moment, and then inhaling slowly. Have them keep one hand on their chest and one hand on their abdomen to feel the falling and rising motion of their breath emptying and filling their lungs. To further encourage abdominal breathing, suggest that they press one hand down on their abdomen as they exhale and let their abdomen push the hand back up as they inhale deeply. Invite questions and comments, point out your observations of their breathing patterns, and make suggestions for improvement as needed.

    A common complaint is that Diaphragmatic, or Abdominal, Breathing feels unnatural and awkward. Assure your students that breathing like this is like learning to ride with training wheels on a bicycle: at first they are very conscious of having to get the feel of and master the various aspects of their new skill. With practice, riding a bike and Diaphragmatic Breathing become one automatic, continuous motion. The training wheels come off the bike, and there is no longer a need to exaggerate the Diaphragmatic Breathing. They need to be patient. They have had a lifetime of breathing incorrectly; suggest that it will take them a while to learn to breathe correctly.

6. Skip to number four of the Deep Breathing exercises on page 27 of the workbook. Assure people that it is all right to breathe through their mouth if they are unable to breathe through their nose. Then have your students practice instruction number five of the Deep Breathing exercise for a few minutes.

7. Instruct your students to continue practicing Deep Breathing while you tell them about the importance breathing plays in their lives. This is a good time to go back to the introduction on breathing that you skipped.

8. Begin to draw the breathing exercise to a close by suggesting they do numbers six through nine of the Deep Breathing exercise. Then ask your students to take a moment to stretch and come back into the room. Invite questions and comments.

Note: This can be the natural point for a break or end of class.

Breathing To Release Tension

Purpose: To relax. While people almost always find Diaphragmatic, or Deep Breathing, very relaxing, they find that their minds begin to wander after a few minutes—to daydreams, worries, memories, or plans—and they forget to deep breathe and relax. The following two exercises provide a focus for the mind.

Time: 10 minutes per exercise

1. Breath Counting

   A. Explain and demonstrate (count your exhalations aloud up to four and begin again at one). State that it's all right if their minds wander. In fact, it is to be expected. When they catch themselves straying from counting their exhalations, they are simply to bring their minds back to "one" as they exhale. Always invite questions before moving on to the practice, since no matter how clearly you explain this exercise somebody doesn't get it.

   B. Have your students take everything out of their laps, uncross their legs and arms, close their eyes if they like, breathe diaphragmatically, and practice this exercise for five minutes.

   C. Invite questions and comments about their experience and the technique.

   Note: This is a favorite exercise among students that is easy to learn and gives some immediate release of tension. If you only have a brief amount of time to devote to breathing, you might want to include this exercise after instruction seven of Deep Breathing above. There is a more detailed breath counting meditation in the Meditation chapter of the workbook.

2. Letting Go of Tension

   A. Explain and demonstrate this exercise (think out loud). Invite questions about the instructions.

   B. Have your students practice this exercise for five minutes.

   C. Invite questions and comments about their experience and the technique.

Enlivening Breathing Exercises

Purpose: These exercises can be done alone or in any combination for the purpose of energizing the group. You may choose to teach these exercises together, or to save them and dole them out when everyone's attention seems to be drifting.

Time: Each exercise takes less than 5 minutes to learn and practice.

Space Requirement: The Windmill and Bending exercises require people to stand, unencumbered by chairs, at least an arm's length apart.

Instructions:

1. Begin by teaching Complete Natural Breathing and the Purifying Breath, following the instructions on pages 28 and 29 of the workbook. Assure people who cannot breathe through their nose that it is all right to breathe through their mouth for these exercises.

2. Then go on and teach one or both of the following exercises: The Windmill and Bending described on pages 29 and 30 of the workbook.

3. Suggest that people practice these exercises when they need a lift at home or at work.

Optional Breathing Exercises

- Abdominal Breathing and Imagination is a sample of how breathing techniques can be combined with mental pictures to enhance energy, reduce pain, and assist in the healing process.

- Alternative Breathing is extremely relaxing and particularly effective in relieving tension and sinus headaches. The one problem with this exercise is that it requires relatively clear nasal passages. Have people do this exercise as slowly and gently as they can. It is unlikely class members will do this exercise unless you demonstrate it to them, because the instructions, while simple, appear complex.

- Breath Training for people who hyperventilate.

- Controlled Breathing describes how to make a breath training tape.

Special Notes

1. Demonstrate each of the breathing exercises as you describe them.

2. Repeat the instructions two or three times while people are practicing these exercises.

3. Walk around the room and identify and correct obvious problems individuals are having.

4. At the completion of each exercise, answer questions about that exercise before going on to the next one.

Audiotape

The New Harbinger Publications 18-minute cassette tape *Breathing* is divided into four segments, which you can use to teach the following exercises:

1. Deep Breathing

2. Two short energizing breathing exercises

3. Complete Natural Breathing

4. Alternative Breathing

4

Progressive Relaxation

Exercise: Progressive Relaxation

Purpose: Deep relaxation without the aid of imagination or will power. All it takes is simple, mechanical tensing and relaxing of major muscle groups.

Time: about 30 minutes

Instructions:

1. The instructions in the workbook on pages 35 to 38 are quite complete.

2. *Optional:* You can use the 22-minute audio cassette *Progressive Relaxation* by New Harbinger Publications to take the class through Progressive Relaxation. This way you are free to demonstrate the technique as the tape describes what to do. You are also able to walk around the room during the exercise and correct individual problems.

3. *Optional:* You can model your own presentation of Progressive Relaxation from the audio cassette. This will help you establish proper timing.

Special Notes

While Progressive Relaxation can be practiced in a chair, it is best to practice in a recliner, bed, or on a comfortable rug or blanket on the floor. The reason is that when you instruct a person to let go, they ideally should be able to let go without worrying about hitting a hard surface, hurting themselves, placing their hands on their legs, or making a loud noise. Make clear to your students sitting in chairs that they are learning this technique in a less than ideal setting, and that it will be much easier to do at home.

You will need to move around the room and observe each person practicing this exercise in order to make corrections.

The most obvious mistake that people make when they are first learning this technique is to slowly bring their arms or legs down. This is an indication that they are not letting go of the tension in their arms. This is easily corrected by you demonstrating, using exaggeration, "letting go" of your arm tension in a *controlled* slow way and then "letting go" by letting your arm fall *limply* to your side. Immediately let them try to do it correctly.

Encourage people who do not tense enough to tense more, and suggest to those who are obviously overly straining to tense less.

Tell class members to be cautious with any part of their body that has been previously injured or is otherwise weakened. Pain is an indication that they are tensing too hard.

Reassure people that tingling, jerking, needlelike sensations, "surging," and warmth are all normal sensations associated with tensing and relaxing.

After you have taken the group through the basic procedure of Progressive Relaxation, have participants form dyads for three minutes of sharing. Answer questions when the groups combine into one.

Encourage people to practice Progressive Relaxation twice a day for 15 minutes. Almost all participants express some immediate benefit from this exercise, and within a week or two most people report attaining profound relaxation in less than 15 minutes.

Have group members keep track of their level of tension on the 10-point scale described on page 21 in the workbook before and after they do Progressive Relaxation at home.

Once people have mastered the long form of Progressive Relaxation (this usually takes a week or two), have them practice the short form twice a day.

When students have mastered the short form of Progressive Relaxation, suggest that they use it at times during the day when they are tense: when they are waiting, during a mini work break, before they start driving, after a stressful interaction, or before they go to sleep.

This is a powerful relaxation exercise and easy to learn. It should be included in any abbreviated stress management program.

5

Meditation

Introduction

Purpose: Meditation can be a profound form of deep relaxation for the mind as well as the body in which the individual attempts to focus his attention on one thing at a time.

Time: 5 minutes

Instructions:

1. See pages 39 and 41 in the workbook.

2. As with breathing, it is more important for people to experience meditation than understand it intellectually. However, unlike with breathing, focusing on one thing at a time seems foreign and difficult to Westerners. So a brief introduction to meditation will help to familiarize your audience with the fundamental elements common to all forms of meditation, the historical background of meditation, and the scientifically proven benefits of it.

Environment: People can practice meditation on the floor, on cushions, or in chairs. Soft lighting and a comfortable room temperature are ideal. A quiet atmosphere is preferred, but not necessary. Suggest that extraneous sounds are part of the natural environment to be noted and then let go of.

The exercises in the workbook are divided into five groups.

Group 1. Three Basic Meditations

Time: 30 minutes

Instructions:

1. At the very least, you will want to teach your students how to establish their posture, to center themselves, to assume a passive attitude, and to do the three basic meditations. Instructions are on pages 41 to 46 in the workbook.

2. At the beginning of the meditation exercises, let people know that should they feel particularly uncomfortable with one of the exercises, they can modify the instructions, or simply stop doing it. They can just sit and relax until the exercise is over. If necessary, they can get up, go outside and walk around. Encourage people to try the exercise again on their own, after they have had an opportunity to sort out their discomfort and to ask questions.

3. The Breath Counting Meditation is an ideal exercise to begin with, because it builds on the students' recently acquired knowledge about breathing and therefore seems familiar. It is easy and it is deeply relaxing.

4. Then teach Mantra Meditation. Remind the students that they can use any sound they feel comfortable with for the mantra. Have them chant "OM" aloud as a group for a few minutes. Then have them repeat their mantra to themselves for a few minutes. Ask participants to compare for themselves the difference in their body between chanting aloud versus in silence. Ask which is more relaxing?

5. In teaching the Gazing Meditation, you may choose to furnish some items to contemplate, such as a blue glass vase, a candle, an abstract carving, or a natural object. Have the large group break into small circles, so that participants can gaze at one of these items from a comfortable distance. Or you may prefer people to contemplate something that they brought with them, such as a pin, ring, or coin. In this case, nobody has to move.

   Typical problems that people encounter with Gazing Meditation include:

   - **Eye strain.** Reassure students that it is all right to blink. Remind them not to stare at the object, but rather softly explore it with the eyes. Some people prefer to take out their contact lenses when they do this exercise. Do not do this exercise for more than five minutes at first. Suggest increasing the time on this exercise, but only as comfortable.

   - **Visual illusions.** Most people react to these with interest, some with alarm. Explain that illusions are common and that they are to be noted and then let go of rather than become distracted by them.

6. Review Special Considerations on page 46 of the workbook.

7. Form small groups of three or four to let people discuss their experiences with these meditation exercises. Which did they enjoy the most and why? What difficulties did they encounter? How did they deal with them? After five minutes, have the group assemble into one group and let each small group representative give a brief summary of the important points and questions brought up. Address any unresolved questions or problems.

8. Suggest that your students select one of these forms of meditation to practice 10 to 20 minutes, once or twice a day for a week, and then decide if they want to continue this form of meditation or try another.

Group 2. Releasing Muscular Tension

Time: up to 5 minutes each

These exercises are essentially Body Awareness exercises. You may choose to include them when you discuss Body Awareness. They are optional meditation exercises. See the instructions in the workbook on pages 46 and 47.

Group 3. Softening

Time: up to 5 minutes each

The first of the three exercises in this group is especially useful in suggesting a way to deal with uncomfortable feelings and sensations that are bound to come up during meditation, or for that matter, any time. The other two exercises are variations on the same theme and are optional. See the instructions in the workbook on pages 48 to 50.

Group 4. Being Present in the Present

These are three optional exercises that teach the individual to focus his attention on the here and now. These exercises can be practiced anywhere, but for best results they initially should be practiced with minimal disturbances. The instructions for these exercises are simple to follow. They are in the workbook on pages 50 to 53. You may choose to do the Walking Meditation with the class, if you have the space. Ideally, you can suggest that individuals try these meditations on their own in their daily life and then report back to class in the next session what their experiences were like.

Group 5. Letting Go of Thoughts

Time: 5 minutes

This is a powerful exercises that teaches the individual to observe his flow of consciousness without becoming caught up in it. It underscores the unruly nature of our minds: how thoughts and sensations appear seemingly from nowhere and become all-consuming if we let ourselves dwell on them. It is suggested as an optional exercise because most people find it difficult, and a few don't stay with it long enough to experience its benefits. The instructions for this exercise are on page 53 of the workbook.

Special Note

Suggest to your students that they can gradually expand the practice time of each of these exercises as feels comfortable.

Audiotape

The New Harbinger cassette tape *Meditation* is 38 minutes long. It is based on the first edition of *The Relaxation & Stress Reduction Workbook* and does not closely adhere to the Meditation chapter in the fourth edition. It includes the following ten segments:

1. Introduction to Meditation
2. Posture, Centering, Scanning for Tension, and Letting Go
3. Yoga Awareness Exercise
4. Problem Solving
5. Breath Counting
6. Mantra Meditation
7. Contemplation
8. Yantra Meditation
9. Lotus of a Thousand Petals
10. Visualizing One Thing at a Time

6

Visualization

Introduction

Purpose: This chapter would have been better named "Imagination," for it describes how to use all of your senses to tap your own creative resources for guidance, healing, stress reduction, and relaxation.

Time: 5 minutes

Instructions:

1. See pages 55 to 57 in the workbook.

2. When introducing this topic, you will probably want to mention some of the fascinating work of Emil Coué, Carl Jung, Stephanie Matthews, O. Carl Simonton, and others. Briefly describe the three different kinds of visualization for change, as well as the rules for effective visualization.

Basic Tension and Relaxation Exercises

Present the three basic tension and relaxation exercises: Eye Relaxation, Metaphorical Images, and Creating Your Special Place; and the two optional exercises: Finding Your Inner Guide and Listening to Music.

1. Eye Relaxation (Palming)

Time: 5 minutes

Instructions: See pages 57 and 58 in the workbook.

Note: Many people assume that they are not imaginative and therefore will perform poorly on the visualization exercises. This is a good visualization exercise to begin with, because it does not rely on imagination. Rather, it allows the individual to relax and observe natural phenomena. Hence, it's almost impossible for anyone to "fail" with this exercise.

2. Metaphorical Images

Time: 8 minutes

Instructions: See page 58 in the workbook.

Note: Here is a slight variation on the instructions given in the workbook. Have your students describe to themselves an uncomfortable place in their bodies which they would like to make feel better. Tell your students to select a tension image that really captures the essence of their tense or painful area. (For instance, a burning, stabbing sensation might bring to mind a sword of dry ice.) Then instruct your students to come up with an image that will greatly reduce or eliminate the tension or pain. Finally, let the two images interact so that the image of tension or pain is diminished, or gotten rid of, by the image of relief. For example, sun shining brightly on the sword of dry ice as it evaporates. Have your students share their images in groups of four or ask for examples in the large group.

3. Creating Your Special Place

Time: 10 minutes

Instructions: See pages 59 to 60 of the workbook.

Note: Tell your students that their special place may be a real place where they have experienced feeling completely relaxed and safe; or it can be a creation of their imagination. Also mention that they may see, hear, taste, smell, and feel their special place in detail, or they may just have a strong general sense of being there. What is important is that they experience and enjoy their special place in their own unique way.

4. Finding Your Inner Guide

Time: 8 minutes

Instructions: See page 60 of the workbook.

Note: This is an optional exercise. While everybody seems to have a positive response to their special place, some people are frightened or saddened by this exercise. This latter group of individuals typically imagine guides who are dead or not to be trusted. Thus, it's a good idea not to combine the two exercises the first time that you teach Creating Your Special Place.

The value of tapping into one's inner guide cannot be underestimated. The people who have difficulties with Finding Your Inner Guide will either work them through or discontinue using this exercise.

An alternative to Finding Your Inner Guide that does not generate negative feelings is Receptive Visualization, found on page 56 of the workbook. Tell your students that they must be patient with these exercises, and may have to practice them for a while before receiving any guidance.

5. *Listening to Music*

Optional Instructions: See pages 60 to 61 of the workbook.

Note: Because listening to music is such an important and easy way to relax, you will want to introduce your students to various types of relaxing recorded sounds, including natural sounds. You can play music before and after class and during breaks. You can use soft background music while teaching some of the relaxation exercises or while your students are filling out questionnaires. Let your class know what you are playing and where they can purchase it. If invited, your students will quickly expand your knowledge of "relaxing sounds."

Special Notes

1. You need to reiterate to your class the three suggestions (A, B, and C) on page 61 of the workbook. The remainder of this chapter is optional.

2. Laughter is an excellent form of tension release. In addition to the humor exercise suggested on page 61 of the workbook, you may want to demonstrate the power of humor by telling a few jokes, sharing an amusing human interest story, or playing part of an audiotape of one of your favorite comics. Encourage your students to look at the humorous side of their problems.

3. A creative outlet can relieve stress and tension. Many adults put aside playing music, writing, painting, or doing crafts long ago in lieu of meeting obligations and getting ahead. The exercise, taken from *Drawing on the Right Side of the Brain*, is a good homework assignment that will demonstrate the relaxing effect of the creative process. It is described on pages 64 and 65 of the workbook. Ask your students who have a creative outlet how it affects their tension level. Suggest to them that they take up an old creative interest, or discover a new one for themselves.

Audiotape

The New Harbinger Publications 21-minute cassette tape on *Imagination* is based on the first edition of *The Relaxation & Stress Reduction Workbook* and does not closely adhere to the chapter in the fourth edition. Use it to get additional ideas for Visualization exercises. Play portions of it for your students in lieu of taking them through the Visualization exercises yourself. It is divided into the following segments:

1. Introduction to Imagination as a stress reduction relaxation tool

2. Metaphorical Images

3. Change pain by pushing it away or changing its size or shape

4. Body scan for tension which is red, and relaxation which is blue; turn all to blue

5. Images of warmth for relaxation

6. Putting down the tension and stress in your life on a mountain path on the way to your special place

7. Active remembering and then letting go

8. Finding an ally

7

Applied Relaxation Training

Introduction

Purpose: This is a progressive program that teaches the individual to relax both mind and body in stressful situations in only 20 or 30 seconds.

Time: 6 to 14 weeks of twice daily practice

Instructions:

1. See pages 65 to 74 in the workbook.

2. Briefly describe the purpose of Applied Relaxation Training, why it was developed, and its six stages (see pages 65 and 66 in the workbook).

3. Since this is a progressive program, it is very important that the individual master one stage before moving on to the next. It takes about a week or two of twice daily practice to become comfortable enough with one stage to feel ready to move on to the next.

4. At the beginning of each session, check in with the individuals in your class regarding their experience with their home practice. If they do not feel comfortable with the stage that they have been practicing, review the stage with them, address any problems or questions they still have, and then encourage them to continue practicing it until they are ready to move on to the next stage. If you are not under time constraints and you sense that your class needs more practice on a particular stage, do a class practice on that stage and postpone teaching the next stage.

5. You can read and/or memorize the appropriate text from Chapter 7 in the workbook to teach the six stages of Applied Relaxation Training. You can instruct your students to do the same for their home practice.

6. *Optional:* You can make an audiotape of the relaxation exercises in each of the six stages of Applied Relaxation Training based on the text in the workbook. You can use this tape in teaching the six relaxation exercises to your students. You can recommend that your students make their own home practice tape based on the text in the workbook.

7. *Optional:* Use the audiotape *Applied Relaxation Training* published by New Harbinger Publications to teach the six stages. Recommend to your students that they purchase their own copies of this tape for home practice.

Stage 1: Progressive Relaxation

1. Use the Basic Procedure on pages 36 and 37 in the workbook. Also see page 67 in the workbook.

2. Have your students do two 15-minute home practices a day.

3. Remind your students that their goal is to relax their entire body in one 15-minute session.

Stage 2: Release-Only Relaxation

1. Use the text on pages 67 and 68 in the workbook.

2. When your students have completed the relaxation exercise, be sure to go over the recommendations in the last three paragraphs of page 68.

3. Have your students continue their twice-a-day daily practice, and suggest that they will be ready to move on to the next stage when they can relax their entire body in one five-to-seven minute session.

Stage 3: Cue-Controlled Relaxation

1. Use the text on pages 69 and 70 in the workbook.

2. Have your students continue their twice-a-day daily practice. Suggest that they rate how relaxed they become, using the 10-point scale on page 21 of the workbook. Tell them that they will be ready to move on to the next stage when they can relax their entire body using cue-controlled relaxation in two to three minutes.

Stage 4: Differential Relaxation

1. Use the text on pages 70 through 72.

2. Remind your students to allow the rest of their body to remain relaxed as they move one part of their body.

3. Have your students continue their twice-a-day daily practice. Suggest that their goal be to relax fully in 60 to 90 seconds in each of the suggested settings before moving on to the next stage.

Stage 5. Rapid Relaxation

1. Use the text on pages 72 and 73 in the workbook.

2. Underscore that this stage is to create the habit of checking in with oneself many times a day, noting any symptoms of anxiety or tension, then relaxing deeply.

3. The goal of this stage is to relax in 30 seconds in natural and nonstressful situations. Save the stressful situations for Stage 6.

Stage 6: Applied Relaxation

1. Give some examples of the body's early warning signs of stress and then ask your students for examples of their early warning signs.

2. Use the text on pages 73 and 74 in the workbook.

3. Take your students through the three-step exercise on page 73 after they have jogged in place vigorously. Invite questions and comments.

4. Take them through the same exercise after they imagine a stressful situation and start to get in touch with their distressing feelings. Invite questions and comments.

5. Describe how to use Applied Relaxation in a real-life stressful situation. Invite questions and comments.

Special Considerations

1. Use the text on page 74 in the workbook.

2. Encourage your students to create the habit of scanning their body for tension and practicing the rapid relaxation technique at least once a day.

8

Self-Hypnosis

Introduction

Purpose: Self-hypnosis can be used as a form of deep relaxation, using positive suggestions to enhance stress management and personal goals.

Time: 15 minutes

Instructions:

1. Give about a five-minute introductory lecture based on pages 75 to 77 in the workbook and then invite questions to further clarify what hypnosis is and is not, what hypnosis can and cannot do.

2. Invite people to briefly describe their experiences and concerns with hypnosis. You can use the positive descriptions to underscore the many ways that hypnosis can be applied. You can use negative descriptions to clarify and allay fears and reservations regarding experiencing hypnosis now. In addition to the section entitled Your Previous Experience With Hypnosis on page 77 in the workbook, here are two other common concerns of people new to hypnosis:

   - "I don't think that I can be hypnotized."
     Acknowledge that this might be so. Assure them that even a light trance or relaxing state can be beneficial; and that with practice, most people find that they can enter trance easily.

   - "Hypnosis is against my religion," or "I fear I will be given an immoral suggestion under hypnosis."
     In both of these cases, the person views hypnosis as evil or dangerous. Give the person the option to leave the room while you do the induction or to stay and observe so that he can become knowledgeable about hypnosis. This leaves the door

open, and perhaps at some future time, with more information and trust, the person will be willing to give hypnosis a try.

Convincer Exercises

Purpose: These are simple exercises that demonstrate to the novice that the subconscious mind, responding to simple suggestions, can take over automatic muscle movement and allow the individual to respond without conscious effort.

Time: Each of these "convincers" takes no more than 5 minutes.

Space: Have your students stand at least an arm's length apart.

Instructions:

1. Two examples of convincers are Postural Sway and Postural Suggestion, found on page 78 of the workbook.

2. Have your students stand, then take them through these two exercises.

The Self-Induction

Purpose: The best way to introduce your students to hypnotic induction is through a demonstration in which they experience a light to medium trance.

Time: 30 minutes

Instructions:

1. Briefly describe the various elements of a self-hypnotic induction (see Personalized Self-Induction on pages 78 to 80 in the workbook).

2. Before starting the induction, have your students select a word or phrase such as "relax now" or "peaceful, safe, and warm" or anything else that has a pleasant and relaxing connotation; for example, their favorite color or place. Tell participants that they will have an opportunity to use this key word or phrase during the induction.

3. Read the Basic Self-Induction Script on pages 80 to 81 in the workbook, or play the 15-minute induction on side 1 of the audiotape *Self-Hypnosis*, published by New Harbinger Publications.

4. When you have completed the induction, return to your normal voice.

5. Suggest that participants get up and stretch. It is best not to do this exercise at the end of a session. Give people ample time to come out of their trance. You may want to call a five-minute break. Encourage people to get up and walk around.

6. With a large group, have people break into groups of four to discuss their experience with this exercise. Get them thinking about how they can improve your induction to fit their particular needs. Have them share what was most and least compelling about the induction for them. Have them ask any questions that come to mind. Have one

person from each group report any interesting comments or unanswered questions to the large group. With a small group, have each person share in turn.

7. After you have dealt with any unanswered questions, go over the key rules for a successful self-induction (see page 80 of the workbook).

Abbreviated Inductions and Five Finger Exercise

Purpose: These are mini-relaxation exercises that create feelings of calm and alertness. The Five Finger Exercise is useful for people who have low energy, are depressed, or are suffering from low self-esteem.

Time: These inductions take less than five minutes to teach, and only moments to perform once a person becomes proficient with self-hypnosis.

Instructions: The shorthand techniques, such as the "pencil drop," described on pages 82 and 83 are optional.

Hypnotic Suggestions

Purpose: Many symptoms of stress are a result of learned habitual responses to stress. Once in a relaxed state of mind, a person is more suggestible. This is an opportunity to suggest new ways of responding to old stresses.

Time: 15 to 30 minutes

Instructions:

1. Go over the rules for hypnotic suggestions on pages 83 and 84 of the workbook. Then have your students write hypnotic suggestions for the 14 problems listed on page 84 of the workbook.

2. Have them compare their answers with those in the workbook on pages 85 and 86.

3. Have them write down at least three of their own problems and then write hypnotic suggestions for each one of them.

4. *Optional:* If you do not have time to do this exercise in class, you can suggest that your students do it as homework.

5. Whether this exercise is a class or homework assignment, you will need to give your students an opportunity to correct their errors on the hypnotic suggestions applied to their own problems. This can be done in groups of four, followed by the reporter from each group bringing up comments or questions when all groups come together. If your group is small, have each person share in turn.

6. *Optional:* You can go over the first several problems in the workbook with the class as a whole. Ask for hypnotic suggestions from class members for each of the problems. Quickly shift to asking for real problems from the class. Ask for hypnotic suggestions

for each of these problems. With this option, you are able to immediately explain errors, and to give some additional good examples.

7. Suggest as homework that your students write and audiotape their own self-induction, and to include one or more of the hypnotic suggestions dealing with problems they want to work on. Tell them to listen to this tape once a day for a week, and report back on their experience.

Self-Hypnotic Induction for a Specific Problem

Purpose: This optional exercise on pages 87 to 89 of the workbook outlines how to use self-hypnosis as part of a general plan to resolve a particular problem. The specific problem used in the example is insomnia.

Time: 5 minutes to 1 hour and 50 minutes

Instructions (Options):

1. Give a brief lecture, using the example in the workbook, to explain how an individual needs to analyze his problem, define his goal, change external factors if he can, and work on irrational and stressful thoughts before he is ready to create positive auto-suggestions and a self-induction (5 minutes).

2. Follow Option 1 with the Basic Self-Induction Script with the Sleep Induction (20 minutes).

3. Follow Option 1 with an exercise in which each individual selects a problem to work on and writes out the answers to the following questions at home or in class. Invite questions in the large group or have your students break into dyads to review each other's answers to questions A through G so that they can give each other constructive feedback on questions B, E, D, and G (50 minutes).

    A. What is your specific problem?

    B. What is your goal?

    C. What external factors are contributing to your problem?

    D. What can you do to eliminate or change each one of these external factors so that they no longer contribute to your problem?

    E. What positive suggestions can you create for your induction that take into account each one of these external factors?

    F. What are you saying to yourself that is irrational, distressing, and/or nonproductive that contributes to your problem?

    G. What positive suggestions can you create for your induction that take into account each one of these negative thoughts?

4. After your students have completed Option 3, give them the homework assignment to write an induction tailored to their particular problem, incorporating their goals and other positive auto suggestions. Recommend that they review the sections of the

workbook on Personalized Self-Induction, Basic Self-Induction Script, and Hypnotic Suggestions. Have them slowly read their induction in a monotonous tone of voice into a tape recorder and then play it back to themselves so they can experience it. If they do not have access to a recorder, they can have someone else read it to them. If they like, they can further refine their induction by building in more of the suggestions that they find most effective and eliminating the ones that are least effective (5 minutes).

5. Following Option 3, have your students write out their positive auto suggestions about their goal and so forth in the order in which they would like to hear them in an induction. Show your students where they can insert their positive auto suggestions into the Basic Self-Induction at the point designated on page 81 in the workbook (5 to 10 minutes).

6. Following Option 5, have your students read their induction into a tape recorder and then listen to it, or have someone read it to them for homework. Remind them to speak in a slow, monotonous tone of voice and repeat each suggestion at least three times (2 minutes).

7. Following Option 5, have your students break into dyads. Have one person slowly read in a monotone the Basic Self-Induction Script plus the other person's list of positive auto suggestions as the other person experiences the trance. Remind the reader to repeat each suggestion at least three times. Have the person who experienced the trance consider which suggestions worked best for him and which he would want to change. Reverse roles, and repeat (45 minutes).

Special Considerations

These points can be made at the conclusion of your presentation on self-hypnosis or addressed as they come up during the presentation. Be absolutely sure that you cover the first point involving safety!

Audiotape

The New Harbinger Publications cassette tape *Self-Hypnosis* covers all the major points in the workbook chapter. Most important, it includes two inductions that demonstrate the nonverbal aspects of self-hypnosis such as tone of voice, cadence, and pauses.

Side 1, which is 27 minutes long, includes:

- Introduction to Self-Hypnosis

- Exercises on Postural Sway and Postural Suggestion to demonstrate the power of suggestion

- Fifteen-minute induction

- Five rules on how to do effective inductions

Side 2, which is 30 minutes, includes:

- Four ways to deepen an induction
- Ten-minute induction, incorporating the four deepening techniques
- Abbreviated inductions
- How to create and use hypnotic suggestions

9

Autogenics

Introduction

Purpose: Autogenic training is a systematic method of relaxation, using auto suggestion.

Time: 30 minutes

Materials: For students without a workbook, a list of autogenic phrases.

Instructions:

1. See pages 91 through 94 of the workbook.

2. Give a brief historical introduction to Autogenics.

3. Explain briefly the physiology of each of the basic six verbal formulas for physical regulation.

4. State the contraindications as well as benefits.

5. Explain and give examples of:

   - The three basic Autogenic Training (AT) postures

   - Settling into a position that is comfortable for you

   - Passive concentration

   - Silent, steady repetition of the verbal formula

   - Use of visual, auditory, and tactile images to enhance the verbal formula (e.g., arms made of lead, warm sun, steady metronome, or child's swing)

   - Returning to the formula when distracted

   - Autogenic discharges

- Ending an AT session with "When I open my eyes I will feel refreshed and alert"

  Make sure your students are not still in a trancelike state as they move on to their regular activities.

6. Have your class practice this brief version of the first stet AT verbal formulas. The fifth and sixth verbal formulas are not included for brevity's sake and because they can be problematic for certain people.

   - Both of my arms are heavy.

   - Both of my legs are heavy.

   - My arms and legs are heavy.

   - Both of my arms are warm.

   - Both of my legs are warm.

   - My arms and legs are warm.

   - My heartbeat is calm and regular.

   - It breathes me.

7. Instruct your students to say to themselves the first line four times, taking five seconds each time and pausing three seconds between each recitation. Have them do the same for each of the lines. Demonstrate the pace, as the class practices.

8. Give your students a typed version to refer to as they go through the formulas on their own if they do not have their own workbook.

9. In a small group, invite each student to talk about his experience. In a large group, have one person from each of the small groups summarize comments or questions.

10. Suggest that they practice this brief version at home at least twice a day for a week.

11. Remind class participants that this is not how Autogenics is traditionally taught, and that if they are interested in approaching it more systematically, they can follow the 12-week program in the workbook on pages 95 to 98 or attend an Autogenics Training Workshop.

12. Once the students have mastered the basic six verbal formulas for physical regulation, they are ready to try the Meditative Exercises briefly described in the workbook on pages 98 to 100.

Audiotape

The New Harbinger Publications cassette tape *Autogenics* is 37 minutes long and goes through the 12-week program described in the workbook. It would be worth your while to listen to part of it to get a sense of the pacing used for saying the verbal formulas.

10

Brief Combination Techniques

Introduction

Purpose: Therapists have found that many of the techniques already presented have a more profound effect when combined.

Instructions:

1. See pages 101 through 107 in the workbook.

2. Self-explanatory.

Special Notes

While all these exercises can be used for relaxation, the following are a few suggestions as to other purposes they can serve.

- Exercises for quick relaxation:

  1. Stretch and Relax

  2. Autogenic Breathing

- Exercises for thought stopping:

  3. Stop and Breathe

  4. Changing Channels

- Exercises to enhance self-esteem and mood:

  5. I Am Grateful

  8. Breath Counting

  10. Accepting Yourself

- Exercises to enhance sense of self-control:

   6. Deep Affirmation

   9. Taking Control

- Exercises to reduce pain and tension:

   7. The Tension Cutter

11

Recording Your Own Relaxation Tape

Introduction

Purpose: To explain and demonstrate how students can make relaxation tapes tailored to their own particular needs.

Time: 30 to 40 minutes

Instructions:

1. See pages 109 to 115 in the workbook.

2. Self-explanatory.

3. This is an optional topic.

4. Demonstrate how you record your voice as you take your students through a relaxation exercise. You may choose to use part of the Relaxation Script on pages 111 to 114 in the workbook. At the end of the relaxation exercise, be sure to suggest that when they open their eyes and return to the room they will feel relaxed, refreshed, and alert. When they open their eyes, encourage them to stretch and move around. Call for questions and comments. You may want to schedule a short break.

5. Play back a brief section of what you recorded. Ask class members what they think are the ingredients of a good relaxation audiotape. Follow this discussion with any additional suggestions that have not been covered.

12

Biofeedback

Introduction

Purpose: To show how biofeedback brings to conscious awareness subtle biological processes for the purpose of self-regulation and relaxation.

Time: 20 to 40 minutes

Instructions:

1. See workbook pages 117 to 125.
2. Self-explanatory.
3. This is an optional topic.
4. Describe the basic principles of biofeedback.
5. Describe who is likely to benefit from biofeedback.
6. Describe the basic types of biofeedback used for relaxation training.
7. Point out a few examples of how a person can be aware of biofeedback without the aid of a machine: pulse, skin temperature, sweat, and breathing.
8. If possible, bring in biofeedback equipment and demonstrate its use during a relaxation exercise. At the very least, bring in food, fish tank, and/or indoor-outdoor thermometers so that a few of the students can use them as you take the group through a relaxation exercise.

Special Notes

The great majority of people learn to relax using the relaxation techniques already presented. A small number of people, however, fail to alleviate a symptom of tension despite using standard relaxation techniques. These people may very well benefit from biofeedback training, in addition to learning relaxation techniques.

Some people believe that they can become even more relaxed with biofeedback training. Others do not trust their abilities to relax on their own, and believe that a machine might help. For these individuals, it is particularly important to hear the merits and limitations of biofeedback.

13

Thought Stopping

Introduction

Purpose: This technique eliminates nonproductive and unpleasant thoughts. It is one of the easiest stress management techniques to learn. Your students will report a high level of success with it.

Time: 25 minutes

Materials: A timer with an alarm, rubber bands (optional).

Instructions:

1. Briefly describe this technique, its origin, and the various explanations for its success (see pages 127 to 128 of the workbook).

2. State clearly what kind of thinking it works best in eliminating: nonproductive, unrealistic, self-defeating thoughts that waste your time and make you feel bad.

3. The Stressful Thoughts Inventory on workbook pages 129 to 131 is optional. Most people know instantly what you are talking about and can identify a number of such thoughts that they would like to get rid of.

4. Follow steps 2 through 5 of Thought Stopping in the workbook on pages 131 and 132.

5. Suggest other types of thought substitution that work well:

   • A pleasant fantasy or memory completely unrelated to the stressful thought.

   • An activity such as whistling or singing, or getting up and walking around.

Thought substitution can be described as "changing the radio station when you don't like what you are listening to."

6. Review the special considerations on pages 132 and 133 of the workbook with your students.

7. Tell them to work on only one stressful thought at a time. It is important that they make an agreement with themselves at the onset to use thought stopping every time they catch themselves having the stressful thought.

8. Point out to your students that by following the instructions, a stressful thought can be neutralized within a few days. This does not mean that a person will never have the stressful thought again. But it does seem to lose its power and occur much less frequently. Occasionally, a person will have to use Thought Stopping more than once on an old stressful thought that reappears.

9. Answer questions in the large group.

Audiotape

The New Harbinger cassette tape *Thought Stopping* is 20 minutes long. It explains the technique and goes through steps 2 to 5 in the workbook. It even has varying timed intervals of silence for dwelling on the stressful thought and signals for when to stop.

14

Refuting Irrational Ideas

Introduction

Purpose: Rational Emotive Therapy (RET) reduces stressful emotions and physiological arousal by identifying a person's irrational, extremely negative self-talk and changing it to rational, appropriate, and less extreme self-talk.

Time: 1 hour

Materials: At least one copy of the homework sheet on page 151 in the workbook for each student. They can make additional copies from their workbook or from the copy that you give them.

Instructions:

1. Briefly describe the basic tenets of RET as outlined on workbook pages 135 to 137.

2. Some people take an hour or more to fill out and score the Belief Inventory on pages 138 to 143 of the workbook. Have your students do it as homework or skip it.

3. You will need this time to give a lecture including at least the first 10 of the 21 irrational ideas. Explain why they are irrational and extreme, and give examples of less extreme and more appropriate ideas for each irrational idea (see pages 143 to 147 in the workbook).

4. Conclude this lecture with the Rules to Promote Rational Thinking on pages 147 and 148 of the workbook and then answer any questions.

5. Walk your students through steps A through E for Refuting Irrational Ideas in the workbook on pages 148 to 152. Go over the homework example. Then call for an example from students and take the class through steps A through E again.

6. Give class members the homework assignment to spend at least 20 minutes a day doing this exercise, using examples from their daily lives. Suggest that they make copies of the blank homework sheet to fill in for their convenience.

7. At the beginning of the following session, have the students go over their homework in groups of four. Have them each share one example of steps A through E and get corrective feedback from their particular group. Then have one member of the group report back to the large group any interesting comments or questions. If you have a small group, have each student share in turn.

8. After you deal with unanswered questions in the large group, you may want to review the special considerations on page 152 of the workbook.

9. Tell your students to get into the habit of asking themselves, "What am I feeling?" and "What am I telling myself about this situation?" whenever they have an extremely negative emotional response to a situation. In this way, they will learn to identify their irrational self-talk, have an opportunity to mentally go through this homework assignment, and to tell themselves something less extreme and more appropriate that will generate less stressful emotions.

Rational Emotive Imagery

Purpose: Use imagination to change excessively unpleasant emotional responses to stressful events into less intense, more appropriate emotional responses.

Time: 30 minutes

This technique is not as complicated and time-consuming to teach as Refuting Irrational Ideas. If you are pressed for time and can teach only one of the cognitive techniques, you may prefer to try this one.

Instructions:

1. Briefly go over the five steps for Rational Emotive Imagery with the class, using an example. See pages 152 and 153 of the workbook.

2. Have the class take a few minutes to get into a comfortable position and relax.

3. Take students one step at a time through the five steps again, instructing them to focus on a stressful event of their own. Give them ample time to use their imagination to transform their original response to their stressful situation to a more appropriate one.

4. When they are through, have them write down their original emotions, their new emotions, and what they changed in their belief system in order to get from one to the other.

5. Have participants share their experiences in groups of three or four. The people in the small group can offer suggestions for alternative beliefs to assist an individual who had difficulty shifting from the more extreme to the less extreme emotions. Have one person report back to the large group with any unanswered questions.

6. Go over the three levels of insight necessary to change habitual emotional responses. These insight levels are listed at the bottom of page 154 of the workbook.

7. As a homework assignment, you can suggest that your students practice Rational Emotive Imagery 20 minutes a day for a week. On page 153 of the workbook is a list of sample situations and alternative emotional responses. You can ask your students to fill in their own stressful situations, along with their stressful and more appropriate emotions, on page 154. They can use this list to practice Rational Emotive Imagery.

15

Coping Skills Training

Introduction

Purpose: This technique allows the individual to practice responding to a stressful event in a relaxed manner, using Guided Imagery, Progressive Relaxation, Deep Breathing, and Stress Coping remarks.

Time: 5 minutes

Instructions:

1. A good way to introduce this topic is to describe a few anecdotal stories of stressful situations in which people typically respond with symptoms of anxiety. Ask for a few examples from individuals in the class.

2. Explain how anxiety is a learned response to a stressful situation, and that it is possible to learn how to respond to the same situation in a relaxed manner.

3. Briefly describe how Coping Skills Training teaches greater self-control (see pages 157 and 158 of the workbook).

Learning To Relax Efficiently

Introduce Coping Skills Training after your students have already mastered Progressive Relaxation and the basic breathing techniques.

Making a Stressful Events Hierarchy

Time: about 15 minutes

You may want to ask your students to do the hierarchy as homework, since some people will need much longer. Alternatively, you can have people finish their hierarchy at home.

Materials: at least two pieces of paper and a pen or pencil

Instructions: See pages 158 to 160 of the workbook.

Note: You may want to tell your students to limit their stressful situations to those they are likely to encounter often, so that they will have ample opportunity to practice their Coping Skills. Once they have mastered Coping Skills, they are likely to spontaneously apply them to infrequent stressful situations.

Applying Relaxation Techniques to Your Hierarchy

Time: 10 to 15 minutes

Instructions: Have your students get into a comfortable position and relax, using Progressive Relaxation and Deep Breathing. Follow the instructions on page 160 of the workbook.

Stress Coping Thoughts

Time: 15 minutes

Materials: paper and pen or pencil

Instructions:

1. See pages 160 through 163 in the workbook.

2. Give a brief lecture on the four elements of an emotional response, with emphasis on thought. Show how the feedback loop can create a vicious circle: negative thoughts to stressful physical reactions to stressful behavioral choices to more negative thoughts. Explain how Stress Coping Thoughts can create a feedback loop that leads to a sense of self-control and relaxation.

3. Go over the examples of Stress Coping Statements under each of the four categories in Meichenbaum and Cameron's stress inoculation program.

4. Have your students think of one of their stressful situations in which they would like to respond with greater self-control and relaxation. Tell them to write it at the top of their paper. Under this, have them write the first category: **Preparation.** Halfway down the page, have them write the second category: **Confronting the stressful situation.** On the other side of the paper, have them write: **Coping with fear;** and halfway down the paper: **Reinforcing success.**

5. Have your students fill in Stress Coping Statements for each of the four categories appropriate for their specific stressful situation. While they can use examples from the workbook, they should come up with at least two of their own Stress Coping Statements for each category.

6. Have your students get into a comfortable position; relax; and then imagine going through their stressful situation, using their coping statements.

7. Have individuals share with the group their most effective coping statements that they have made up for themselves. Have the group offer suggestions to individuals who are having difficulty coming up with effective coping statements.

8. Tell your students to memorize their Stress Coping Statements and/or have this list ready to use when they are most likely to find themselves in their stressful situation. When first learning this skill, they can review these statements just before they are about to encounter their stressful situation.

9. Suggest to your students that they may want to practice using this skill with their stressful situation in front of a mirror, on video or audio recorder, or with a friend as an intermediate step before trying them out in vivo.

Coping "In Vivo"

Instructions: Once your students have learned to respond in a relaxed manner, using progressive relaxation and deep breathing, to their stressful situations when they imagine them, and once they have memorized their stress coping statements, they are ready to apply these skills to real-life situations. Some setbacks are expected. But with practice, relaxation and stress coping thoughts will become the automatic response to stressful situations and physical sensations. See the example on pages 163 to 165 in the workbook. Here are a few suggestions for your students to help them with this phase of the training:

1. If possible, begin using the relaxation techniques before entering the stressful situation. Otherwise, use the first hint of physical or emotional distress as a cue to relax.

2. Remember to breathe. Slow, deep natural breaths are ideal, but just remembering to breathe while going through your stressful experience will help significantly.

3. At first, rehearse the coping statements just before entering the stressful situation. Keep a list of them handy.

4. Use coping statements while going through the stressful situation.

5. Afterwards, review how it went. Add coping statements to combat aspects of the stressful situation that were not previously taken into consideration. Replace ineffective old statements with more potent ones.

6. Practice these skills often to make them automatic. This is why it is important to select stressful situations that occur frequently.

16

Goal Setting and Time Management

Introduction

Purpose: The key assumption in this chapter is that to effectively manage your time, you must learn to structure your life around what is most important to you, and to minimize the time you spend on activities that you do not value. Vilfredo Pareto's 80-20 principle is a good way to start thinking about what is most important and what is not.

This chapter teaches you how to clarify your values, define your goals, and develop a plan for reaching them; it invites you to look at how you currently use your time and bring it into closer alignment with your priorities; it gives you tips on how to combat procrastination and more efficiently organize your time.

Time: 5 minutes

Instructions: Give a brief lecture based on pages 167 and 168 in the workbook.

Clarifying Your Values

Time: 30 minutes

Materials: two pieces of paper and a pen for each student

Instructions:

1. See pages 169 to 170 in the workbook.

2. Define values, give some examples of values, and explain why clarifying one's values can be useful.

3. Before you take your class through the guided fantasies, have them clear their laps, get into a comfortable position, close their eyes, and get relaxed. After you have read to them the first scene, give them a few minutes to reflect on it before you have them open their eyes and write their answers. Repeat this process for the second scene. In the large group, or small groups, ask people to share what they learned from this exercise. *Optional questions to ask your students:* Did it confirm what you already knew about yourself? Any surprises? Did your priorities change or stay the same for both scenes?

4. After you have explained the importance of ranking values from the most to least important to them, have your students do it.

Setting Goals

Time: 30 minutes

Materials: one or two pieces of paper and a pen for each student

Instructions:

1. See pages 170 to 173 in the workbook.

2. Define goals and how they differ from values. Explain why it is important for their goals to reflect their values. (3 minutes)

3. Go over the five questions under Designing Effective Goals on page 171 that people should ask themselves as well as Balancing Your Goals. Have your students take notes if they do not have the workbook. (5 minutes)

4. Go over the example of how Eric used his list of values to guide him in writing his goals. (5 minutes)

5. Have your students write down at least one goal for each of their values. This is a good homework assignment, or you can give your students at least 15 minutes to work on it in class.

Developing an Action Plan

Time: 1 hour

Materials: one piece of paper (two if they do not have the workbook), a pen, and a blank copy of the Self-Contract for each student

Instructions:

1. See pages 173 to 177 in the workbook.

2. Explain why an Action Plan is so crucial to achieving one's goals. Outline what an effective Action Plan includes. Have your students take notes if they do not have a workbook.

3. Describe the two strategies used to create an Action Plan: *1. Imagine that you have already achieved your goal* and *2. Brainstorming.* Use the examples from the book; or better, ask for examples from your audience to illustrate these 2 strategies.

4. Go over the process of Evaluating Your Progress. Encourage your students to choose a support person with whom they can review their progress. If they don't have one, suggest that they mark on their calendar when they plan to review how they are doing.

5. Explain the Self-Contract. While this may seem corny to some people, research shows that it increases the likelihood of people following through on their goals.

6. Have your students design an Action Plan, using one of the two strategies you have suggested.

7. Have your students write out a Self-Contract based on their Action Plan.

Evaluating How You Spend Your Time

Time: 1 hour class time; 3 days to keep Time Log at home

Materials: two pieces of paper and a pen for each student

Instructions:

1. See pages 177 to 182 in the workbook.

2. Explain how to keep a Time Log. You can use Samantha's Time Log as an example. If you have the option of having your students keep a Time Log for three days and your students are likely to comply, fine. If not, have your students do an estimate of their Time Log.

3. Have your students go over their Time Log, using the system described under Evaluating Your Time Log, and write down the changes they would need to make it more consistent with their values and goals.

4. Invite your students to briefly share (in the large group or in small groups) how they would be willing to change their behavior so that it is more consistent with their values and goals.

Combating Procrastination

Time: 15 minutes

Materials: one piece of paper (two, if they do not have the workbook) and a pen for each student

Instructions:

1. See pages 182 to 184 in the workbook.

2. Have your students write down three situations in which they typically procrastinate.

3. Give a lecture on Combating Procrastination. If your students do not have a copy of the workbook, suggest that they take notes.

4. Have them list a few appropriate suggestions for combating each of the situations in which they typically procrastinate and try them out at home. If possible, be sure to follow up on this home practice assignment at the beginning of the next session.

Organizing Your Time and Organizing Your Day

Time: 20 minutes

Materials: one piece of paper and a pen for each student if they don't have the workbook

Instructions:

1. See pages 184 to 186 in the workbook.

2. This is what most people think the purpose of time management is: by being better organized, one can get more done. This section can be taught independent of the other sections of this chapter. If you are teaching an abbreviated module on time management, it is best to include these two sections.

3. Give a lecture on this topic. If your students do not have a copy of the workbook, recommend that they take notes. Invite questions and comments.

17

Assertiveness Training

Introduction

Purpose: How a person relates to others can be a significant source of stress. Assertive communication allows the individual to set limits and express what he wants, feels, and believes while taking into account the rights and feelings of others. This tends to minimize interpersonal strain.

Mini Assertiveness Course

Time: This is a topic that can easily be expanded into a course all its own. How can you possibly teach Assertiveness Training in an hour or two? If you are pressed for time, here is a suggested outline that you can cover in an hour to an hour and a half.

Instructions:

1. *Optional:* Have your students fill in the blanks in response to the six problem situations presented on workbook pages 187 and 188. As they answer these questions, they will become more curious about assertiveness. (5 minutes)

2. Introduce Assertiveness Training (see pages 187 to 191 of the workbook). This may include a list of Mistaken Traditional Assumptions versus Your Legitimate Rights. The list of basic assumptions regarding your rights (on pages 189 and 190 of the workbook) is optional in this abbreviated presentation because it is so time-consuming (at least one-half hour). (5 to 8 minutes)

3. Define aggressive, passive, and assertive communication (see page 191 in the workbook). Test your students' ability to distinguish these three styles of interaction by

asking them to label the six scenes presented on pages 191 to 193 as aggressive, passive, or assertive. A quick and fun way to do this exercise is to read aloud the first scene, ask for the correct label from a student, and then ask why he chose that particular label. If the label is incorrect, ask if someone else had another label and why he chose that label. Proceed through the other five scenes in this manner. (15 to 20 minutes)

4. *Optional:* Have your students go over their answers to the questions on pages 187 and 188 in the workbook and label their responses as aggressive, assertive, or passive. Ask them if their answers tend to fall predominantly under one label? (5 minutes)

5. *Optional:* Instruct your students to fill out column A only of The Assertiveness Questionnaire on workbook pages 194 to 196. They can fill out column B at their leisure. (5 minutes)

6. Teach your students the Short Form Assertiveness Technique on pages 202 to 203 of the workbook. Note that this is the same as steps three, four, and five in Your Script Change on page 198 of the workbook. Demonstrate the Short Form Assertiveness Technique. (10 minutes)

7. Instruct participants to write an assertive message for one of their problem areas. They can refer back to the items they checked off on The Assertiveness Questionnaire to identify a problem area. (5 minutes)

8. In groups of three, have each individual briefly state the "when," the "who," and the "what" of their problem situation and then state their assertive message. The other group members can give constructive feedback about the assertive message. Does it include the three elements: "I think," "I feel," and "I want"? Is it clear? Is it complete? Does it avoid blame? Allow about 5 minutes per group member to present his problem situation and assertive message, and to receive feedback. (15 minutes)

When you call the large group back together, ask for questions and comments. (5 to 10 minutes)

Long Form

Instructions:

1. Have your students respond to the six problem situations on pages 187 to 188 of the workbook. You may choose to read the situations and have your students answer on a blank sheet of paper, to make copies of the problem situations available for your students to write on, or have your students answer these questions from their own workbooks at home or in class.

2. Introduce Assertiveness Training (see pages 187 to 189 of the workbook). (5 minutes)

3. Go over the Mistaken Traditional Assumptions versus Your Legitimate Rights.

- You may choose to lecture on this topic (see pages 189 to 190). (30 minutes)

- You may give this as a homework assignment and then divide the class into groups of four to talk about the beliefs people held as children versus as adults. To focus discussion, ask people to comment only on those Legitimate Rights they have difficulty accepting as adults. (15 minutes)

- You can ask a class member to take a Traditional Assumption position and defend it for a minute. Then ask another student to take the position of the juxtaposed Legitimate Right and defend it for a minute. You can demonstrate how to do this, using the first Traditional Assumption and Legitimate Right in the list. Explain that this may take some play acting for people who are defending positions that they themselves do not hold. As soon as the first Traditional Assumption and Legitimate Right has been presented, move right on to the next. Take questions and comments at the end. (30 minutes)

4. Describe the Three Basic Interpersonal Styles on page 191 of the workbook.

   - Test your students' ability to distinguish these three styles by asking them to label the six scenes presented on pages 191 to 193. See Instruction 3 in the Mini Assertiveness Course of this *Leader's Guide* for suggestions regarding structuring this exercise.

   - Have your students go over their answers to the questions on pages 191 and 193 of the workbook. Follow the instructions in the short form.

5. Tell your students to fill out the Assertiveness Questionnaire on pages 193 to 196 of the workbook. This can be done as homework or classwork. (10 to 15 minutes)

6. Explain and demonstrate how to do a problem scene. Have your students write out a description of two to four of their problem scenes, using the instructions on pages 196 to 197 of the workbook.

   - This can be done as homework or class work.

   - Have students break into groups of four in which each person presents one example of a problem scene and the other three give constructive feedback. You may want to have people underscore the criteria for a good problem scene on the bottom of page 197, or write these criteria on a blackboard for the small groups to refer to. Have one person report back any interesting comments or unanswered questions when the large group reconvenes. (30 minutes)

7. "Your Script for Change"

   - Instructions: See pages 198 to 202 in the workbook.

   - Go over the six steps in the "LADDER."

   - Explain the difference between a poor and good LADDER by using examples.

- Have individuals write an example of a LADDER based on one of their problem scenes.

- Break the large group into groups of four, and have each individual present his LADDER and get constructive feedback from the other three people.

- Have a spokesperson from each of the small groups bring any interesting comments or questions back to the large group. This is an important opportunity for you to correct any major misconceptions.

- Demonstrate how to use the LADDER in a role play between yourself and a class volunteer, or set up a role play between two students, using one of their LADDER scripts.

- Mention the five basic rules for assertive body language (see pages 203 to 204 of the workbook).

- Have each individual in the same small groups role play their LADDER with one other person, while the other two members observe and then give feedback. The other person in the role play can give valuable information about what it was like to be on the receiving end of the LADDER.

- Have a spokesperson from each of the small groups bring any interesting questions or comments back to the large group.

- Mention to the group that the LADDER is a valuable tool to use when a person is faced with a major problem scene that he can anticipate, such as asking his boss for a raise or setting limits with a friend. It is also good to use in problem scenes where the individual has a long established pattern of responding nonassertively. In such cases, he can anticipate the problem coming up again, and can think through and rehearse his new assertive response.

- Have your students practice this technique as homework at least twice and report back. Further role playing and feedback may be necessary to address problems that have come up.

8. Short Form Assertive Technique

   - Instructions: See pages 202 and 203.

   - Point out to your students that the Short Form Assertive Technique is identical to three of the elements in "Your Script for Change":

   "Define the problem" is the same as "I think"

   "Describe your feelings" is the same as "I feel"

   "Express your request" is the same as "I want"

   - Demonstrate this technique to the class in a role play, and then have your students practice in groups of four.

- Have your students practice this technique as homework. (30 to 40 minutes)

9. Learning How To Listen

  - Instructions: See workbook pages 204 to 206.

  - Explain assertive listening.

  - Demonstrate assertive listening in a role play.

  - Have students break into groups of four to role play assertive listening. The person who is listening should request the speaker to play the role of someone that the listener would have difficulty listening to in real life.

  - Have the spokesperson from each small group report back to the large group any interesting comments, problems, or questions.

  - Have your students practice this technique as homework. (30 to 40 minutes)

10. Arriving at a Workable Compromise

  - Instructions: See pages 206 to 207 in the workbook.

  - Explain Workable Compromise.

  - Demonstrate Workable Compromise.

  - Have your students go back to their problem scenes of their LADDER and think about the best way for them to arrive at a Workable Compromise for each one of these scenes.

  - Have your students role play Workable Compromise with one other person, with two people observing and coaching.

  - Have your students practice this technique as homework. (30 to 40 minutes)

11. Avoiding Manipulation

  - Instructions: See pages 207 to 209 in the workbook.

  - Explain each of the seven techniques for dealing with manipulation, giving a brief demonstration of each as you go.

  - Mention that two of the dangers in using Content-to-Process Shift are inaccurately reading the other person's mind and appearing condescending.

  - Point out that Defusing and Assertive Delay are basically other ways of saying "time out" when you realize the conversation is going nowhere.

  - Note that Assertive Agreement, Clouding, and Assertive Inquiry are three ways of dealing with critics.

  - Go over the typical blocking gambits that are used to block assertive requests. Give examples of each and of how to deal assertively with each.

- If you decide to have your students take the time to practice any of these techniques in class, the Broken Record and the techniques for dealing with criticism are the most important. (at least 15 minutes)

Special Note

When you have four to five hours, you can teach everything in the Assertiveness Training chapter in the workbook. Ideally, you should have at least twice that much time, spread out over four to eight weeks. Assertive behavior change involves interacting with significant people in an individual's life. It is helpful when the person can practice an assertive technique during role play in class, and follow this up with an "in vivo" homework assignment. He then can return to the next class session to report on and fine-tune his newly acquired assertive skill. It is also useful when the individual can read and reflect on the Mistaken Traditional Assumptions versus Your Legitimate Rights so that he is more conscious of what he believes, why he believes as he does, and how this affects his behavior. Finally, it saves class time when students can fill out some of the questionnaires as homework, to be discussed in a later class.

18

Job Stress Management

Introduction

Purpose: Even if most of the people in your class are homemakers or full-time students, they may be suffering from the burnout that comes from chronically not feeling in control of their lives. They would benefit, therefore, from tools designed to empower them. This is the central theme of Job Stress Management.

Time: 5 minutes

Instructions: See pages 211 and 212 of the workbook.

Ten Steps Toward Managing Your Job Stress

Step 1. *Identify Your Symptoms of Job Stress*

Time: 8 minutes

Materials: If this is done as class work, you may choose to make copies of the inventory for people to fill out, read the questions and have them write their answers on a blank piece of paper, or have them read the questions from the book.

Instructions: See pages 212 and 213 in the workbook.

Step 2: *Identify the Sources of Your Job Stress*

Time: 10 minutes

Materials: Either have your students use their own workbook or give them copies of this inventory along with a blank piece of paper for their answers.

Instructions: See pages 213 to 216 of the workbook.

Step 3: Identify How You Respond to Your Specific Job Stressors

Time: 40 minutes

Materials: paper and pen

Instructions: See pages 216 to 219 of the workbook.

Note:

- This is a good homework assignment. Students may want to take notes during their workday or at the end of the day.

- Have students review their response to stressors in groups of four.

- Answer questions.

Step 4: Set Goals To Respond More Effectively to Your Job Stressors

Time: 30 minutes

Materials: piece of paper and pen

Instructions:

1. See pages 219 and 220 in the workbook.

2. Give your students 10 to 15 minutes to write a contract.

3   Have students review their contracts in groups of four for 10 to 15 minutes.

4. Answer questions when the large group reconvenes.

Step 5: Motivate Yourself

Time: 5 minutes

Materials: paper and pen

Instructions:

1. See pages 220 and 221 of the workbook.

2. Have your students write several ways that they can reward themselves for working on and achieving their goals.

3. Tell your students to write a more preferred activity that they can use to motivate themselves to do a less preferred activity.

Step 6: Change Your Thinking

Time: 1 hour

Materials: paper and pen

Instructions:

1. See pages 221 to 223 in the workbook.

2. After you have explained the three generic thoughts about work that trigger painful emotions, have your students write examples of each from their own lives on a piece of paper.

3. After you have explained how to cope with the three stressful generic thoughts, have your students write coping statements for each of their stressful thoughts that fall in this category. Then answer any questions.

4. After you have explained how to change or adapt to work stressors, have your students write how they will do this for each of the statements they wrote under this category. Then answer any questions.

5. After you have suggested that class members consider their options and the risk of pursuing these options, have them write options and risks involved for each thought they listed under the third category. Then answer any questions.

6. Have your students meet in groups of four and share one generic thought and its coping statement from each of the three categories. Answer questions when the large group reconvenes.

Step 7: Deal With Your Boss

Time: 30 minutes

Materials: paper and pen

Instructions:

1. See pages 224 and 225 of the workbook.

2. Have your students write answers to the six questions on page 224 of the workbook. Suggest that a good time to talk with their boss is at the time of their annual review. If that is a long way off, they can set up a special time to talk with him or her.

3. After you have explained why it is important to understand what motivates bosses, have your students write responses to the three parts of the exercise on pages 224 and 225 of the workbook. Then have your students share their answers with four others and also get feedback and suggestions.

Step 8: When in Conflict, Negotiate

Time: 45 to 60 minutes

Materials: paper and pen

Instructions:

1. See pages 225 and 226 in the workbook.

2. Explain and demonstrate, using role playing, the four steps of negotiation.

3. Have your students write a script to negotiate an office conflict, using this four-part model.

4. Divide your class into groups of four. Let each person take a turn at role playing their script with one other person in the small group. The two observers can act as coaches. At the end of the role play, have the small group discuss what was good about it, as well as what could be improved.

5. Have the small group reporter share any interesting comments and ask questions when the large group reconvenes. Answer any questions.

Step 9. Pace and Balance Yourself

Time: 15 minutes

Materials: paper and pen

Instructions:

1. See pages 226 and 227 in the workbook.

Additional points

2. Have your students read this section, and then write specifically how they could apply each of the eight suggestions to their lives. If an item does not apply, have them write N/A. This can be done as a homework assignment.

3. Have them share their answers in groups of four.

4. Suggest that they apply these ideas to their daily schedule.

Step 10. Know When To Quit

Time: Guided fantasy, plus writing: 25 minutes; writing fear and goal statements: 10 to 15 minutes; group interaction: 20 minutes

Materials: paper and pen

Instructions:

1. See pages 227 to 229 of the workbook.

2. *Optional:* Have your students get into a comfortable position. Lead them in a five-minute relaxation exercise.

    After they are relaxed, suggest that they imagine themselves in their current job five years from now without anything substantially changed about their job. Ask them: "What do you see . . . hear . . . feel? Are you happy? Are you doing what you want? Are you where you want to be?" Tell them, "Let that image go for now."

    Ask them, "What would it take to make your current job more enjoyable or satisfactory?" Tell them to imagine their job with these changes. Ask what it would take to make these changes happen. Tell them to let that image go for now.

Ask them: "Describe your ideal job. Include your job title, your job responsibilities, your boss, your co-workers, your environment, and the management."

Tell them: "When you open your eyes, write down how you imagine it will be for you in your job in five years with no changes. Then write down what changes you think would make your current job better for you, and what it would take to make these changes happen. Finally, describe your ideal job."

3. Have them write down their fears about leaving their job. Then tell them to turn these "fear statements" into goals designed to get around the barrier. Give an example of this. Have them share a couple of fear and goal statements in groups of four for the purpose of receiving feedback. Have the small group reporters share any interesting comments or questions when the large group reconvenes.

19

Nutrition

Introduction

Purpose: To give students the opportunity to compare their usual eating patterns with 10 basic rules for positive eating so that they will be motivated to make improvements in the way that they eat.

Time: 3 minutes

Instructions: Describe the value of healthy eating (see pages 231 to 232 in the workbook)

Self-Assessment

Time: no time to three days of homework; 0 to 25 minutes of class time

Materials: for each student (if they do not have the workbook), a blank copy of the Daily Food Diary (from which they can make at least two additional copies), a copy of Sharon's Food Diary, a copy of Sharon's Food Diary Summary, and a blank copy of the Food Diary Summary

Instructions:

1. See pages 242 to 246 in the workbook.

2. Ideally, you can have your students keep a Daily Food Diary for three days as homework prior to a discussion of the principles of healthy eating. Explain that the purpose of keeping this record is to get an exact account of what they are actually consuming, which they can later compare with what nutrition experts consider a balanced diet.

3. Use Sharon's Food Diary on page 243 of the workbook as an example of how to fill out one day of the Daily Food Diary. The first three columns are self-explanatory, but

you still need to remind people to list precisely what they are eating, especially if it contains fat, sugar, or caffeine. The Food Guide Points column is a rough estimate of how to count servings. Go over the bulleted guidelines on page 242 and then use Sharon's Food Diary as an example of how to fill this out. Have your students write down in the Setting column the circumstances in which they were eating and their feelings while they were eating in the Feelings column. The environment in which a person eats and how he feels when eating often influences what he eats. External and internal cues other than hunger often trigger eating. Explain to your students that becoming aware of what they eat as well as what is going on when they eat is the first step toward establishing a healthy diet.

4. At the completion of three days, have your students fill out the blank Food Diary Summary. For each of the three days they kept a food diary, have them add up all the servings in each respective food group. To calculate the *Daily Average* for a food group, add up the servings in days one, two, and three for that food group and then divide by three. They can better compare their Daily Average Servings with the Ideal Servings after they have learned about the Ten Steps to Positive Eating.

5. *Optional:* If you find it necessary to have your students fill out the Daily Food Diary after you have discussed the Ten Steps to Positive Eating, caution your students not to change their eating habits until after they have completed their Daily Food Diary.

6. *Optional:* If it is not possible for your students to keep their Daily Food Diary for three days, have them fill out a blank Daily Food Diary form, describing a "typical day" for themselves. This should take about ten minutes. Then you can give a lecture on the Ten Steps to Positive Eating. Based on their typical day and the Ten Steps to Positive Eating, they can then fill out their blank Your Personal Positive Eating Goals form on page 249 in the workbook.

7. *Optional:* Your students can skip the self-assessment process and simply listen to your lecture on the Ten Steps to Positive Eating. Based on their memories of their usual eating patterns and the Ten Steps to Positive Eating, they can then fill out their blank Your Personal Positive Eating Goals form.

Ten Steps to Positive Eating

Time: 10 to 45 minutes

Materials: for students without a workbook, a copy of the Recommended Pyramid, the Common Pyramid, and Your Fat Scorecard

Instructions:

1. Give a lecture that is geared to your audience that covers the material on pages 232 to 242 in the workbook. You may prefer to give a formal lecture with questions at the end. But particularly if you are working with a small group, it can be more interesting to the audience if you invite questions and comments as you go along.

2. Illustrate your points with pictures such as the Recommended Food Pyramid and the Common Food Pyramid.

3. Involve your audience by having them fill out Your Fat Scorecard. You may want to create Your Sugar Scorecard and Your Salt Scorecard, using the tips to limit these items on pages 234 and 235.

4. Be sure to make the connection between exercise and nutrition as the best way to achieve and maintain ideal weight.

Taking Charge of Your Nutritional Well-Being

Time: 15 minutes (using Options 5 or 6 under Self-Assessment) to 90 minutes

Materials: for each student, a completed Food Diary Summary; for students without the workbook, a blank Personal Positive Eating Goals form, Sharon's Food Diary, Sharon's Food Diary Summary, and Sharon's Goal-Setting Chart

Instructions:

1. See pages 243 to 250.

2. Have your students review Sharon's Food Diary Summary and compare her average servings for each food group against the ideal servings. What are her major problem areas? What might she do to solve each of these problems?

3. Have your students review Sharon's Goal-Setting Chart to see what Sharon identified as her major problems and how she decided to solve these problems.

4. Have your students review their own Food Diary Summary and compare their average servings per food group against the ideal servings.

5. Have your students write down on their blank Your Personal Positive Eating Goals form any food group in which their average servings differ from the ideal servings, the specific problem, and a solution that they would be willing to try.

6. Have your students review the Setting column on Sharon's Food Diary. Ask them to consider whether the circumstances in which Sharon ate might have contributed to unhealthy eating. How might she realistically improve the circumstances in which she eats? Compare the students' answers with the possible alternatives Sharon can use on page 248 in the workbook.

7. Have your students review the Setting column of their own Daily Food Diaries. What about the settings in which they eat? Have them write down their answers in the Problem column of their Your Personal Positive Eating Goals form. How might they realistically improve the circumstances in which they eat? Have them write down their answers in the Solution column of their Your Personal Positive Eating Goals form.

8. Have your students review the Feeling column on Sharon's Food Diary. May her feelings when she ate contribute to unhealthy eating? How might she realistically

improve her feelings? Compare the students' answers with Sharon's answers on page 248 in the workbook.

9. Have your students review the Feeling column on their own Daily Food Diaries. May their feelings when they eat contribute to unhealthy eating? Have them write down their answers in the Problem column of their Your Personal Positive Eating Goals form. How might they realistically improve their feelings when they eat? Have them write down their answers in the Solution column of their Your Personal Positive Eating Goals form.

Final Thoughts

1. Remind your students to make only a few changes in their eating habits at a time, and to give their new habits at least a month to become established before they add any more. Making too many changes at once can be stressful!

2. Suggest that they remind themselves about good nutrition by posting the Recommended Food Pyramid and Your Personal Positive Eating Goals on their refrigerator.

3. Point out the resources on nutrition in the Bibliography at the end of the workbook chapter as well as in their local community.

20

Exercise

Purpose: To provide basic information about how to start and stick with an exercise program.

Types of Exercise

Time: 5 to 10 minutes

Instructions:

1. See pages 251 to 254 in the workbook.

2. Give a brief introductory lecture on the three basic categories of exercise: aerobic, stretching, and toning.

3. Describe the general benefits of exercise, emphasizing that these benefits occur only with a commitment to regular practice.

4. Ask for a show of hands from people who are already engaged in some form of regular exercise. Ask these people with their hands up to leave them up if this includes at least 20 minutes of aerobic exercise at the minimum of three times a week. Ask the people with their hands still up to leave them up if they also stretch and warm up before starting and stretch and cool down afterwards. Explain the importance of warming up and cooling down. If you have time, ask these people what their exercise program is.

5. Give precautions.

Developing Your Own Exercise Program

Sample Exercise Program

Time: about 1 hour

Materials: comfortable clothes and a watch with which to count seconds

Instructions:

1. See pages 262 through 268.

2. Take your students through this sample exercise program.

    A. Modify the length of each part to meet the time restrictions of your class.

    B. Demonstrate as well as describe the proper way to do each stretching and toning exercise before you have your students do it.

    C. Explain target heart rate and how to calculate it. Demonstrate how to take your pulse, using the carotid artery and wrist. Have your students count their resting pulse as you keep time for ten seconds and then have them multiply this number by six.

    D. Assume that your class is out of shape and take them through the three-part progressive aerobic section on page 268 in the workbook. Have your students continue checking their pulse as described in C.

3. *Optional:* Save time by integrating the introduction with this sample exercise program.

Overcoming the Barriers

Time: 30 to 40 minutes

Material: one piece of paper and a pen for each student

Instructions:

1. See pages 254 through 257 in the workbook.

2. Give a few examples of typical barriers to exercise, and then invite your students to share why they can't exercise.

3. *Optional:* For homework, have your students keep a Daily Exercise Diary to uncover all the opportunities they have to exercise during the course of their day, along with their reasons for and against exercising. Use Angela's Daily Exercise Diary on page 255 in the workbook as an example.

4. Confront your students' reasons for not exercising with the questions on the bottom of page 255 and on page 256 in the workbook. Have them turn their "I can't" statements into "I choose not to" statements. Get them to begin to examine and refute beliefs and fears that keep them from exercising. This can be done in the large group, using examples from the workbook and the class.

5. In an individual writing exercise, have your students respond to their reasons for not exercising. Use the example on page 257 in the workbook: Responses to Reasons for Not Exercising. If you have a small group, ask each student to share a couple of his reasons for not exercising and his responses in turn. Give corrective feedback. Be sure

that everyone gets the concept of this exercise. If you have a large group, have your students give each other feedback in groups of two or three, and then report back to the large group with unanswered questions and with comments.

Choosing the Best Type of Exercise for You (Optional)

Time: 10 minutes

Materials: If your students do not have their own workbook, give them copies of pages 258 and 259 in the workbook.

Instructions:

1. See pages 256, 258 to 259, and 260 to 261 in the workbook.

2. Have students who are unsure about what form of exercise they want to try fill in the blanks on pages 258 and 259 in the workbook.

3. Have your students read about the pros and cons of different types of aerobic exercise on pages 260 and 261 in the workbook.

Establishing Goals

Time: 15 to 30 minutes

Materials: For students who do not have a workbook, a copy of the Sample Contract Form on page 177 and a copy of the Exercise Diary on page 271 in the workbook.

Instructions:

1. See pages 259 and 262 in the workbook.

2. Give a brief lecture describing the basic ingredients of exercise goals. You may want to include some of the ideas from Goal Setting and Time Management, Chapter 16 in the workbook. There is an example of developing an action plan to accomplish a goal involving exercise beginning on the bottom of page 174 in the workbook.

3. Have your students fill out a self-contract describing their exercise goals.

4. Suggest that they keep an Exercise Diary.

Special Considerations

Time: 15 to 30 minutes

Instructions:

1. See pages 269 through 272 in the workbook.

2. Invite your students to give examples of additional opportunities to exercise and/or list the examples on page 269 in the workbook.

3. Give a brief lecture on Avoiding Injury. Invite questions and comments.

4. Most people have difficulty sticking with an exercise program. Keeping at It and Some Final Thoughts have some good suggestions for your students on how to make their exercise program a permanent part of their lives. Give a brief lecture on these points. Invite questions and comments.

21

When It Doesn't Come
Easy–Getting Unstuck

Introduction

Purpose: To explore why some people are not doing the homework, not applying stress management and relaxation techniques to their daily lives, or not experiencing symptomatic relief.

Instructions:

1. See pages 273 to 276 in the workbook.

2. This topic is optional.

3. Briefly present, in lecture form, the major points in this chapter. You may choose to have your students read the workbook chapter as homework before your lecture.

4. Have your students discuss, in small groups of four, how some of the ideas presented in this chapter might apply to their situation and what they might do to change.

5. Take questions and comments when the large group reconvenes.

Special Notes

The danger of this chapter is that it places the responsibility for change and symptomatic relief on the individual. This can motivate the individual to initiate change from within, rather than wait for a miracle from without. Or it can make a person feel guilty or resigned if he is still unable to relieve his symptoms after significant effort.

It is important for the individual to be patient and to practice these techniques before deciding whether they are beneficial. If symptoms persist after a sincere effort, the individual should seek professional one-on-one help.

22

Homework

Objective

Homework is an essential part of a stress management class or workshop. It is important because:

1. It allows the student to integrate intellectual concepts and techniques into his experience.

2. Only then can the student decide which concepts and techniques are useful to him, and which are not.

3. Through repetition, a new behavior that was at first awkward will begin to feel natural.

4. If the student repeatedly experiences positive feedback in practicing a new behavior, he is likely to continue doing it long after the stress class is over.

Motivation

A major task of the stress management and relaxation instructor is to motivate students to do their homework. In a sense, class time can be looked upon as the time when students come in to get their new homework assignment and report the results of their efforts on the previous assignment. The instructor can enhance homework compliance by

- explaining the purpose of an assignment;
- describing the homework in simple step-by-step instruction orally and in writing;
- demonstrating the homework;

- giving the students an opportunity to practice any new technique in class and to ask questions before practicing it at home;

- suggesting a minimum expectation for performance, with the understanding that the students can exceed this;

- having students keep a written record of their homework progress, along with any comments and questions; and

- providing time at the beginning of the next session to discuss the homework experience and to ask questions.

Reviewing Assignments

Discussion of the previous week's homework assignment shouldn't take more than 20 minutes. In a relatively small group of eight or less students, the instructor may choose to go around and briefly check with each student on his homework experience. Or the instructor may prefer to save time and encourage group interaction by using the small group format to discuss the homework. Certainly in larger groups small group feedback is the most efficient way to discuss homework as well as class assignments. An added bonus of using small groups is that everyone will get an opportunity to speak, including those who are shy.

When you opt for the small discussion groups, you need to provide a clear outline of questions to keep the conversation on track. You may also want to give your students these questions in writing. This is particularly useful for people who arrive late. Typical questions include:

1. Did you meet the minimum expectations of the assignment? Did you exceed the minimum expectations?

2. Do you have any questions about the instructions or your experience?

For those who did the assignment:

3. What did you learn from doing this assignment?

4. What did you like and dislike about the assignment?

5. Do you think that you would benefit from continued practice of the ideas and/or techniques you learned in this assignment? Will you continue to practice them?

For those who did not do the assignment:

6. Briefly, why did you not do the assignment? If something else took priority over your homework, what does that mean to you? Is that something that you want to change? If "yes," how can you make the change?

7. Recall why you are here. Do you think that the homework assignment might help you achieve your purpose for being here?

8. Do you want to do this homework assignment this week? If so, what would you decide to do differently this week?

"No" to Homework

It is important for a person to understand why he does not do his homework assignment, since the reasons he gives will tend to reflect how he maintains his stress patterns.

1. If he rarely says "no" to others, he is devoting most of his energy to others and has little time for himself and stress management homework assignments. He would benefit from the workbook chapters on Assertiveness Training and on Goal Setting and Time Management.

2. If he is a perfectionist, he is likely to set high standards for himself, which he cannot possibly achieve. He may respond to his high standards by not trying, criticizing himself, procrastinating until the last minute, or doing the assignment but not feeling satisfied with his results and not feeling motivated to continue doing the technique beyond the homework assignment. He needs encouragement to set reasonable goals and permission to make mistakes. He would benefit from the workbook chapters on Refuting Irrational Ideas and on Goal Setting and Time Management.

3. If he is an enthusiastic idealist who jumps into the assignment with both feet, he is likely to soon discover that doing the assignment does not net him the instant rewards hoped for. In fact, by practicing a new behavior excessively, he may create new stress in his life. Disillusioned, he loses interest, and stops. Such is the case with people who go on rigid diets or exercise programs. He needs to be reminded that to keep balance in his life he must do all things in moderation and be patient. Progress can be slow. While he needs to work steadily, the rewards will not always materialize as quickly as he would like. He would benefit from the Refuting Irrational Ideas and the Goal Setting and Time Management chapters in the workbook.

4. If he is afraid of new experiences, he will tend to interpret any minor problem as a major obstacle that he cannot overcome. Therefore, he is likely to abandon the exercise. If he becomes anxious or has a stressful thought in the middle of a relaxation exercise, he may assume that it is the fault of the exercise. He needs reassurance from the group leader that he is doing the exercises correctly and that the experiences he is having are normal. He also needs permission to be creative in solving little problems that come up in doing the homework. He would benefit from the Refuting Irrational Ideas and Coping Skills chapters in the workbook.

5. If he believes that self-improvement should not involve effort and inconvenience, he is likely to do the class assignments—but not the homework. He needs to be reminded that his old habits took a long time to form, and it stands to reason that he will have to practice a new behavior for a long time before it becomes habitual and natural. In the meantime, new behavior is going to feel awkward, if not downright uncomfortable. Just because a person knows that exercise is good for him does not mean that he will enjoy exercising at first. Only after he has established an exercise pattern in which he can experience its benefits (e.g., improved mood, concentration, physical fitness and energy) will he be motivated to continue exercising on his own.

6. If he resents being told to do something by anyone, he is likely to resist doing homework assignments. This is a pattern that was probably established early in life, and is unlikely to change in a stress class. As a group leader, take the position that you are responsible for presenting the material, and he can do whatever he likes with it. He is responsible for his own decisions about how he uses his time. If you have good rapport with someone who is oppositional, it is sometimes fun to predict that he won't do the assignment and then be amazed when he does it to spite you. Suggest to people who do not do their assignments and appear not to be improving that one of their options is individual psychotherapy to explore their motivation. Another option is to remind them of their right to stay the same.

7. If he does the homework assignment in a manner that varies significantly from the original instructions, first determine whether the general goal of the assignment was accomplished. If so, compliment him on his creativity and ability to shape the assignment to his own needs. If the general goal of the homework was not reached, point this out and ask him if he is interested in achieving this goal or satisfied with his outcome. If he wants to achieve this goal, have him meet with you or one of the students who was successful with the assignment during the break to go over the instructions and correct his misconceptions.

Here are some additional suggestions for reviewing homework assignments:

- Do not chastise people for not doing their homework. Everybody learns in different ways. Keep in mind that some people will go through the entire class without doing homework and yet appear to benefit from the class. They seem to pick up what they need by attending the class and possibly reading the book.

- When someone is conscientiously doing the assignments and yet continues to have significant symptoms of stress, he should be referred for medical and/or psychiatric evaluation.

- In further structuring the small groups, suggest that the people who did not do the assignment report after the people who did do the assignment. This ensures that those who put out the effort to do homework get corrective feedback.

- While it is useful for the individual to understand why he did not do his homework, this should not become the major focus of small group discussion. A person can simply acknowledge to the group that it was his decision not to do the assignment, why he gave priority to something else, and whether this is indicative of a pattern in his life that he could change if he wanted to. Remind people to change "I couldn't . . . " to "I chose not to . . . . " Then he can decide if he wants to do the assignment during the next week, given his personal needs and priorities.

- Ask one person to volunteer to act as a spokesperson for the small group when the large group reconvenes. This person can share with the large group any interesting comments or unanswered questions that came up in the small group.

• Model clearly defined boundaries. Tell your students that you are their stress management and relaxation consultant who will share the most current concepts and techniques available to help them with their stress management problems. Remind students that they are ultimately responsible for their own well-being. You respect their right to do as they choose with their lives, including the decision to remain the same by not doing anything differently. Part of your own personal stress management is not to take responsibility for decisions that are the responsibility of others.

23

Class Formats of Varying Lengths

One Three-Hour Presentation

I. *Introduction* (20 minutes)

    A. See Chapter 1 of workbook: "How You React to Stress"

    B. What is Stress?

    C. Four Major Sources of Stress

    D. The Fight or Flight Response

    E. Chronic Stress and Disease

    F. Typical symptoms of stress in everyday life

    G. The remainder of this presentation will focus on ways that the average person can gain greater control over the stress in his life.

II. *Take care of your playing piece in the game of life*

    A. Why is it important to take care of your body?

    It is true that your susceptibility to life-threatening illness is largely determined by your ancestry. But while you had no control over who your parents were, you do have some choice about what to do with the body you inherited. Most people who take good care of their bodies say they do so because it makes them feel good and enhances their quality of life. It also makes it easier for them to cope with the daily onslaught of stresses that can slowly wear down a body that is not kept in good condition.

B. Exercise (5 minutes)

1. See Chapter 20 of the workbook.

2. Emphasize the importance of regular aerobic exercise for a minimum of 20 minutes, three to five times a week.

3. Encourage moderation and safety, including warming up and cooling down and stretching before and after.

4. Suggest to your audience that not exercising is a choice. Tell them that for every reason they give themself for not exercising, to give themself a solution to their self-defined limitation. Give a few examples.

5. Make the point that people need to create an exercise program, taking into account their current condition, their tastes, and their personality type. They must choose a form of exercise they like and do it in a way that will be positively reinforced. Give a few examples.

C. Nutrition (5 minutes)

1. See Chapter 19 of the workbook.

2. Stress the Ten Steps to Positive Eating in Chapter 19.

3. If possible, provide your audience with the illustration of the Recommended Pyramid versus the Common Pyramid (see page 232).

D. Relaxation (20 minutes)

1. The Relaxation Response versus the Stress Response (see page 2 of the workbook).

2. Teach the Relaxing Sigh (see pages 28 and 29 of the workbook).

3. Have your participants get into a comfortable position in their chairs. Tell them to take everything off their lap, and then teach Breathing Awareness and Deep Breathing (see pages 25 to 27 of the workbook, and Chapter 3 in this guide). Alternatively, teach Progressive Relaxation.

4. While your participants are still in their relaxed position, have them imagine themselves in their special place (see Creating Your Special Place on pages 59 and 60 of the workbook).

5. Toward the end of this exercise, have them describe to themselves in one brief sentence how they feel in their special place. For instance, "I am warm and relaxed, safe, and at peace."

6. At the end of this exercise, suggest that they now return to the room relaxed, alert, and refreshed. Suggest they practice, on a daily basis, the relaxation exercises they

just learned, as well as carry out their plans to improve their exercise and nutrition programs.

    7. Suggest that people stand up, stretch, walk around, and take a five-minute break.

    8. After the break, answer questions. (5 minutes)

III. *Take charge of your thoughts* (30 minutes)

    A. Explain how "man is not disturbed by events, but by the view he takes of them." See pages 135 through 137 in the workbook.

    B. Go over the Rules to Promote Rational Thinking (see page 147 in the workbook).

    C. Use the exercise Rational Emotive Imagery (see pages 152 to 154 in the workbook) to show your audience how to develop their own strategies for changing stressful emotions by altering their stressful thoughts.

IV. *Take an active stance in shaping your environment*

    A. Tools of effective time management drawn from Chapter 16 of the workbook (40 minutes)

        1. List your one-month, one-year, and lifetime goals.

        2. Write down how much time you spend at each kind of activity you do during the course of a typical day. For example: 8 hours sleeping, 2 hours commuting, 2 hours preparing and eating food, 2 hours watching TV, 1 hour on the phone talking to friends, 1 hour talking to mate, 8 hours working, 10 minutes daydreaming, 15 minutes in the shower, 15 minutes dressing, and 30 minutes shopping.

        3. Compare your current use of time to your important goals. Assign top, medium, or low priority to all of your activities and goals.

        4. Eliminate low-priority items, give minimum amounts of time required to medium-level priorities, and set aside specific time to work on high-priority items.

        5. Allow yourself to do low-priority items only when you have spent your allotted time on the high- and medium-priority items.

        6. Break down high-priority goals into manageabie steps.

        7. At the beginning of the day, make a list of what you plan to accomplish. Review the list at the end of the day. This is an excellent way to learn how much time specific activities really take. Unfinished tasks can be added to the next day's list, or prioritized downward.

        8. Learn to say "no."

        9. Avoid rushing by scheduling ample time for each task you plan to do. Include time for interruptions and unforeseen problems.

10. Set aside several periods each day for quiet time. Arrange not to be interrupted, and focus on a deep relaxation exercise.

B.   Three easy steps to setting limits and asking for what you want (30 minutes)

See Short Form Assertiveness Technique on pages 202 and 203, Chapter 17 in the workbook.

V.   *Summarize your major points and answer questions* (10 minutes)

One-Hour Presentation

This three-hour format can be shortened to a one-hour presentation as follows:

I.   *Introduction* remains the same (15 to 20 minutes)

II. *Take care of your playing piece in the game of life*

A.   Summarize your points about exercise and nutrition in five minutes.

B.   Do a ten-minute relaxation exercise of your choice.

III. *Take charge of your thoughts*

A.   Summarize how "man is not disturbed by events, but by the view he takes of them" in five minutes (see pages 135 through 137).

B.   Go over the Rules To Promote Rational Thinking (see pages 147 and 148 in the workbook).

C.   Give an example of Rational Emotive Imagery to show your audience how to change their stressful emotions by altering their stressful thoughts (see pages 152 to 154 in the workbook).

Save five to ten minutes at the end to summarize your major points and answer questions.

IV. *Take an active stance in shaping your environment*

A.   Summarize the tools of Effective Time Management in ten minutes (see Chapter 16 of this guide).

B.   Summarize the three easy steps to setting limits and asking for what you want in five minutes (see pages 202 and 203 in the workbook).

Ten-Week Class

All the topics in *The Relaxation & Stress Reduction Workbook* can be introduced in a ten-week class, allowing two hours per class. As a general rule of thumb, teach one relaxation exercise and one stress management technique each week. Begin every session, except the first one, by reviewing the preceding week's homework. It is best to do the relaxation exercise next, followed by a short break. You want your participants to be alert when they go home, especially if you are doing a night class. Do an energizing breathing exercise when you sense minds are drifting.

The following is a suggested ten-week Relaxation and Stress Reduction Class format:

Week:	Relaxation Exercise	Stress Management Technique
1	Body Awareness	Introduction
2	Breathing	Nutrition & Exercise
3	Visualization	Thought Stopping
4	Progressive Relaxation	Refuting Irrational Ideas
5	Autogenics	Coping Skills
6	Biofeedback	Goal Setting and Time Management
7	Self-Hypnosis	Assertiveness Training
8	Meditation	Job Stress Management
9	Brief Combinations	Recording Your Own Relaxation Tape
10	Applied Relaxation Training	When It Doesn't Come Easy— Getting Unstuck

12-Hour Workshop in Two Days

Day 1

I. *Introduction* ($1\frac{1}{4}$ hours)

A. Simplify your life and have your students purchase the text, *The Relaxation & Stress Reduction Workbook*, as part of the price of your workshop.

B. See Chapter 1 of the workbook: How You React to Stress and Chapter 1 of this guide: Introduction to Relaxation and Stress Reduction.

C. Introduce yourself, describing your background, especially as it relates to stress management, and why you are teaching this workshop.

D. Hand out an outline of your workshop, listing topics to be covered and when people can expect breaks.

E. Define stress.

F. Describe the four major sources of stress.

G. Explain the "Fight or Flight" Response and the Relaxation Response.

H. Explain the relationship between chronic stress and disease.

I. Exercise: Schedule of Recent Experience (30 minutes)
See pages 5 to 9 in the workbook and see Chapter 1 in this guide.

J. Describe typical symptoms of stress in everyday life.

K. Exercise: Symptoms Checklist (10 minutes)
See pages 9 to 11 in the workbook.

L. Point out that the major purpose of this workshop is to teach techniques for deep relaxation and effective stress management. The benefits of these techniques will only be experienced if your students are willing to practice them regularly once the workshop is over.

(15-minute break)

II. *Take care of your playing piece in the game of life* (1 ¹/₂ hours)

A. Why is it important to take care of your body?

1. Nature versus nurture issue

2. Taking control of what you can

3. Quality of life

4. Better prepared to cope with adversity as well as normal aging

B. Exercise (30 minutes)

1. See Chapter 20 in the workbook and Chapter 20 in this guide.

2. Describe the basic forms of exercise, underscoring the health benefits of regular aerobic exercise for a minimum of 20 minutes, three to five times a week. Also point out the value of gradualism, warming up and cooling off, and stretching.

3. Explain "target heart rate" and how to determine it (see pages 262 to 263 and 268 in the workbook). (5 to 10 minutes)

4. *Optional:* overcoming barriers to exercise

a. Explain how exercising or not is a choice.

b. Have your students write down their typical reasons for not exercising and a solution for each reason (see pages 254 to 257 in the workbook).

c. In the large group or in dyads, have your students share their excuses and solutions, and get some constructive feedback.

d. *Optional:* After explaining how exercising or not is a choice, simply ask individuals for reasons why they don't exercise and for solutions to these problems. (5 minutes)

5. Exercise: setting an exercise goal

a. Explain the basic ingredients of an exercise goal (see pages 259 and 262 in the workbook).

b. Have your students fill out a Self-Contract for their exercise goal (see pages 176 to 177 in the workbook). Invite questions and comments.

c. *Optional:* In the large group or in dyads, have your students share their Self-Contract for their exercise goal and get some constructive feedback.

6. Explain how to keep an Exercise Diary (see page 271).

7. Give suggestions for keeping at their exercise program and avoiding injury (see pages 269 to 270).

C. Deep Relaxation (20 minutes)

Follow the seven suggestions for relaxation described in the One Three-Hour Presentation mentioned earlier in this chapter.

D. Nutrition (30 minutes)

1. See Chapter 19 in the workbook and guide.

2. Give a lecture on nutrition basics.

3. Exercise: Have your students write from memory what they typically ingest during the course of a day, including drugs such as alcohol, nicotine, and caffeine.

2. Exercise: Have your students write down at least three ways that they would like to improve their diet and suggest that they set these as goals for the next two weeks. Ask them to also write down how they will motivate themselves to achieve their nutrition goals. Have your students share their nutrition goals and motivators in groups of three or four. Encourage the small groups to give feedback. Invite questions and comments when the group reconvenes.

(lunch break)

III. *Take an active role in shaping your environment*

A. Tools of effective time management drawn from Chapter 16 of the workbook and pages 86 and 87 in this guide (30-60 minutes)

(10-minute break)

B. Assertiveness training

1. Teach the difference between Aggressive, Passive, and Assertive communication. (30 minutes)

a. Have your students fill in the blank lines on pages 187 and 188 of the workbook.

b. Define and give examples of Aggressive, Passive, and Assertive styles of communication. (See page 191 in the workbook and Chapter 17 of this guide.)

c. Go over the exercise on pages 191 to 193 of the workbook.

d. Have your students go over their answers to the "fill in the blanks" exercise to determine which of the three communication styles they are most likely to use.

2. Three easy steps to setting limits and asking for what you want (30 minutes) (see Short Form Assertiveness Technique on pages 202 and 203 in the workbook).

3. Three easy steps to more effective listening (20 minutes)

      a. See pages 204 to 206 in the workbook and Chapter 17 of this guide.

      b. Point out that this is the Short Form Assertiveness Technique in reverse: listening for "I think, I feel, and I want" in what the other person is saying.

   4. Workable compromise (20 minutes)

      a. See pages 206 and 207 of the workbook.

      b. Explain the concept and demonstrate an example, using role play.

      c. Make clear that arriving at a workable compromise works best when each person has expressed how he thinks and feels about the issue at hand, and what he wants.

      d. Have people break into groups of four where two people practice arriving at a workable compromise at a time.

      e. Take questions and invite comments when the large group reconvenes.

(10-minute break)

   5. Avoid manipulation (30 to 60 minutes)
     See pages 207 to 209 of the workbook and Chapter 17 of this guide.

Day 2

IV. *Take charge of your thoughts*

   A. Explain how "man is not disturbed by events, but by the view he takes of them." (5 minutes)
     (See pages 133 to 135 of the workbook.)

   B. Go over at least the first 10 of the 21 Irrational Beliefs. (30 minutes)
     (See pages 143 to 147 in the workbook and Chapter 14 of this guide.)

   C. Go over the Rules to Promote Rational Thinking. (3 to 5 minutes)
     (See pages 147 and 148 in the workbook.)

   D. Teach steps A through E for Refuting Irrational Ideas. (30 to 40 minutes)
     (See pages 148 to 152 in the workbook and Chapter 14 of this guide.)

(15-minute break)

   E. Teach Progressive Relaxation. (20 minutes)
     (See pages 135 to 138 in the workbook and Chapter 4 in this guide.)

   F. Teach Rational Emotive Imagery. (30 minutes)
     (See pages 152 to 154 in the workbook and Chapter 14 of this guide.)

(5-to-10 minute break)

   G. Teach Thought Stopping. (20 to 30 minutes)
     (See pages 127 to 133 in the workbook and Chapter 13 of this guide.)

(1 hour lunch break)

H. Teach Coping Skills. (1 $^1/_4$ hours)
(See pages 157 to 166 in the workbook and Chapter 15 of this guide.)

(10-minute break)

I. Teach Self-Hypnosis. (1 $^1/_4$ hours)

1. See pages 75 to 90 in the workbook and Chapter 8 of this guide.

2. The following is a time-efficient outline:

   a. Introduction: In describing the benefits of hypnosis, emphasize deep relaxation and increased openness to positive, healthful suggestions.

   b. Address concerns regarding self-hypnosis that people may have from past experiences or the media (see page 77 in the workbook).

   c. Demonstrate suggestibility by taking your class through an exercise on postural sway.

   d. Teach the elements of good hypnotic suggestions. Give several examples of hypnotic suggestions for relaxation and stress management. Have your students write out three suggestions for themselves.

   e. Describe the basic elements of a hypnotic induction as well as deepening techniques.

   f. Take them through the basic self-induction script on pages 80 and 81 in the workbook, which includes the basic elements and deepening techniques that you described.

   g. Invite comments and questions on self-hypnosis.

V. *Summary* (15 minutes)

   A. Highlight the important points that you presented in your introduction the first day.

   B. Show your students how to use the Symptom Effectiveness Chart on pages 6 and 7 in the workbook.

   C. Stress that practice of these techniques on a regular basis for at least a month will help to establish habits of effective stress management and relaxation.

   D. Invite questions and comments.

Other New Harbinger Self-Help Titles

The Anxiety & Phobia Workbook, Second Edition, $15.95
Thueson's Guide to Over-The Counter Drugs, $13.95
Natural Women's Health: A Guide to Healthy Living for Women of Any Age, $13.95
I'd Rather Be Married: Finding Your Future Spouse, $13.95
The Relaxation & Stress Reduction Workbook, Fourth Edition, $14.95
Living Without Depression & Manic Depression: A Workbook for Maintaining Mood Stability, $14.95
Belonging: A Guide to Overcoming Loneliness, $13.95
Coping With Schizophrenia: A Guide For Families, $13.95
Visualization for Change, Second Edition, $13.95
Postpartum Survival Guide, $13.95
Angry All The Time: An Emergency Guide to Anger Control, $12.95
Couple Skills: Making Your Relationship Work, $13.95
Handbook of Clinical Psychopharmacology for Therapists, $39.95
The Warrior's Journey Home: Healing Men, Healing the Planet, $13.95
Weight Loss Through Persistence, $13.95
Post-Traumatic Stress Disorder: A Complete Treatment Guide, $39.95
Stepfamily Realities: How to Overcome Difficulties and Have a Happy Family, $13.95
Leaving the Fold: A Guide for Former Fundamentalists and Others Leaving Their Religion, $13.95
Father-Son Healing: An Adult Son's Guide, $12.95
The Chemotherapy Survival Guide, $11.95
Your Family/Your Self: How to Analyze Your Family System, $12.95
Being a Man: A Guide to the New Masculinity, $12.95
The Deadly Diet, Second Edition: Recovering from Anorexia & Bulimia, $11.95
Last Touch: Preparing for a Parent's Death, $11.95
Consuming Passions: Help for Compulsive Shoppers, $11.95
Self-Esteem, Second Edition, $13.95
Depression & Anxiety Management: An audio tape for managing emotional problems, $11.95
I Can't Get Over It, A Handbook for Trauma Survivors, $13.95
Concerned Intervention, When Your Loved One Won't Quit Alcohol or Drugs, $11.95
Redefining Mr. Right, $11.95
Dying of Embarrassment: Help for Social Anxiety and Social Phobia, $12.95
The Depression Workbook: Living With Depression and Manic Depression, $14.95
Risk-Taking for Personal Growth: A Step-by-Step Workbook, $14.95
The Marriage Bed: Renewing Love, Friendship, Trust, and Romance, $11.95
Focal Group Psychotherapy: For Mental Health Professionals, $44.95
Hot Water Therapy: Save Your Back, Neck & Shoulders in 10 Minutes a Day $11.95
Older & Wiser: A Workbook for Coping With Aging, $12.95
Prisoners of Belief: Exposing & Changing Beliefs that Control Your Life, $10.95
Be Sick Well: A Healthy Approach to Chronic Illness, $11.95
Men & Grief: A Guide for Men Surviving the Death of a Loved One., $12.95
When the Bough Breaks: A Helping Guide for Parents of Sexually Abused Childern, $11.95
Love Addiction: A Guide to Emotional Independence, $12.95
When Once Is Not Enough: Help for Obsessive Compulsives, $13.95
The New Three Minute Meditator, $12.95
Getting to Sleep, $12.95
Leader's Guide to the Relaxation & Stress Reduction Workbook, $19.95
Beyond Grief: A Guide for Recovering from the Death of a Loved One, $13.95
Thoughts & Feelings: The Art of Cognitive Stress Intervention, $13.95
The Divorce Book, $11.95
Hypnosis for Change: A Manual of Proven Techniques, 2nd Edition, $13.95
The Chronic Pain Control Workbook, $14.95
My Parent's Keeper: Adult Children of the Emotionally Disturbed, $11.95
When Anger Hurts, $13.95
Free of the Shadows: Recovering from Sexual Violence, $12.95
Lifetime Weight Control, $11.95
Love and Renewal: A Couple's Guide to Commitment, $13.95
The Habit Control Workbook, $12.95

Call **toll free, 1-800-748-6273**, to order. Have your Visa or Mastercard number ready. Or send a check for the titles you want to New Harbinger Publications, Inc., 5674 Shattuck Avenue, Oakland, CA 94609. Include $3.80 for the first book and 75¢ for each additional book, to cover shipping and handling. (California residents please include appropriate sales tax.) Allow four to six weeks for delivery.

Prices subject to change without notice.